MOVING TO PORTUGAL

Moving to Portugal

Louise & Ben Taylor

BLUE SEA BOOKS

Copyright © Louise Taylor and Ben Taylor 2012

First published 2012 by Blue Sea Books
1 Church Street, Cromer, NR27 9ER, England
http://www.movingtoportugal.org

Printed on demand by CreateSpace

ISBN 978-1478303121

All rights reserved. No part of this publication may be reproduced, stored
in a retrieval system or transmitted by any means, mechanical, photocopying, recording or otherwise, without the written permission of the
publisher.

Cover design: Csernik Előd (csernik@gmail.com)

Contents

INTRODUCTION

In April 2003, my wife and I visited Portugal's Algarve for the first time.

Our determination to see the world at the same time as maintaining a hectic work schedule in London led us to take lots of hurried short breaks and holidays. We always went somewhere different each time. Once we'd been to Portugal, everything changed.

After that, whenever we had some free time, we didn't have to decide where to jet off to; all we wanted to do was return to Portugal – the place that had captured our hearts.

By 2005, we were sure we wanted to live there some day. By 2007 we were starting to make serious plans. In November 2009, we finally boarded a plane on a one-way ticket, ready to begin our new life.

I started a blog, Moving to Portugal, about six months before our departure, and people suggested that I turn the blog into a book. This created a small problem, in that several loyal readers had already followed the story from the start. To make sure that these people could enjoy the book as much as those new to our tale, I came up with the idea of having my wife, Louise, tell the story from her perspective instead.

The book you hold in your hands (whether in paper form, or new-fangled Kindle format), is the result of 18 months of writing, refining and re-writing. Part 1 of the book is my wife's account of our move abroad and our first couple of years in

Portugal. I take over in Part 2, providing some practical information and advice for those considering a move of their own.

I still maintain the blog; you can catch up with our lives in the Algarve at www.movingtoportugal.org.

I hope you enjoy our story, and hope it inspires a few more people to take a leap into the unknown. I frequently say that it was the best thing we ever did.

Ben Taylor
August 2012

PART 1
LOUISE'S STORY

Goodbyes

The leaving party seemed like a good idea at the time. It still seemed like a good idea at 5 o'clock the next morning, as we sat on London's Waterloo station drinking champagne from plastic coffee cups and waiting for the first train home. Where things came unstuck was at 7.00 am. After only an hour in bed, and still able to taste the champagne and Jägermeister, I was roused from my drunken slumber by the persistent ring of the doorbell. My hangover was enormous. My legs refused to stop shaking and a small sob escaped me as I stumbled downstairs. I opened the door to a shockingly bright early November day and a well-dressed family of five.

"Hello, we've come to pick up the bikes we bought on eBay," the mother said. The father glared grimly at my dishevelled appearance.

"Oh, right. Garage." I pointed. "Hang on – keys."

The family marched smartly off towards the garage. I fumbled around trying to find the garage key for a minute then followed them, a heady scent of last night's booze trailing after me. My hands shook noticeably as I undid the padlock. A minute later, the bikes had been dispatched to their new owners and I was safe to retreat into the sanctuary of the house.

Leaving my husband asleep upstairs (I couldn't bear to wake him and allow him to feel as horrific as I did), I made a cup of strong coffee and sat down on the sofa. The doorbell rang again.

"Hello, I'm here to pick up the sofas I bought on eBay," said a small man in overalls, while his van idled across the street.

"Ok, they're just in here."

"Great. Is your husband or anyone at home? I'm going to need some help lifting them."

"Er, no – didn't you bring someone with you?"

"No, it's just me. You couldn't give me a hand, could you?"

And so all hung-over, shaking 5'1" of me spent the next 20 minutes navigating sofas out of the narrow doorway and carrying them across the street.

The rest of the day continued in much the same vein. At midday, five cups of coffee down and still feeling more ill than I have ever felt, I finally had to wake my husband, Ben. I literally had no choice – the man who had bought our bed on eBay was due to arrive and start dismantling it in ten minutes.

At 2.00 pm, I realised that I needed to take the desk apart in order to get it downstairs ready for collection. At 2.02 pm I realised that my toolkit was currently in a container somewhere on the sea between England and Portugal. Luckily, a practical-natured friend saved the day by changing his plans and coming to dismantle the desk with his own tools.

Somehow, we made it through the day. Just two more sleeps in our house and one night in the airport hotel before our new life in Portugal would begin!

*

The final day in our house was spent doing trips to the dump in the enormous hire car (which we had been using since selling our own car a week previously) and saying sad farewells to family and friends. Unfortunately, a small argument with the gatepost of our narrow driveway meant that we kissed goodbye to the hire car deposit.

I also had to visit our big and very yellow storage unit to meet a few more eBay buyers making off with our worldly goods. At the point we left the UK, our unit still contained various things we had yet to sell, which would be listed on eBay from afar and dispatched during trips back to England over the coming months.

Stupidly, I managed to slice my finger open with a rusty razor blade at the bottom of a box just as the last eBay buyer of the day arrived. He paid in cash. Grabbing the notes, I dashed into my local branch of Barclays in order to deposit the money before the bank closed a few minutes later. I failed to notice the sidelong glances of the staff as I quickly filled out the deposit slip. It was only as I reached the counter, covered in drying blood and clutching a wad of bloodstained notes, that it occurred to me how this might look. Thankfully, the cashier accepted the money with no more comment than a raised eyebrow. Perhaps this happens a lot in South London.

Our last evening at home was spent in frantic activity, cleaning the house from top to bottom and trying to fit the last of our possessions into suitcases. Six of our friends came over for dinner and all ended up pitching in, meaning we finally finished everything around 9.30 pm. We had sold most of what we owned and shipped the rest to Portugal a week previously. Thus dinner (Chinese takeaway), ended up being eaten out of its cartons on the floor, with disposable plastic forks. It wasn't exactly fine dining, but it was the last meal we would have in our home of the past seven years and the last with our best friends for some time.

Both Ben and I were choked up when everyone left. It was a strange mix of sadness and excitement, waving goodbye and turning back into our empty home. A few tears were shed, but the excitement soon won and despite the exhausting day's work, it was some time before we managed to get to sleep.

*

The next day was a busy one. We did two final trips to the dump, and then visited a local art shop to drop off a couple of paintings that they had agreed to sell for us. Next, we had to visit a friend and return the duvet and pillows she had kindly leant us since our own bedding had been shipped. Trips to two of Ben's clients followed, before I drove him to Gatwick airport with our cases, where he would check in to the hotel and await my return.

Next I had to take the hire car back, get a cab back to the house and meet the rental agent to return the keys. This done, all that was left was to get the train to Gatwick to meet Ben. On the train to Clapham Junction I phoned the electric and gas companies, giving them the final readings from our meters. I swapped trains at Clapham and finally sat down to relax.

I woke up some time later when my mobile rang. It was Ben, wanting to know where I was. I peered sleepily out of the window. What I saw didn't look like the usual route to Gatwick. I asked a fellow passenger where we were.

"We've nearly arrived at the coast," she assured me with a smile. "Just a couple more stops." I had slept past Gatwick and well beyond.

And so my last evening in England was spent not relaxing in a hotel as planned, but waiting on a cold station in the middle of nowhere for a connecting train. After nearly an hour's wait I was on my way back to Gatwick, standing up the whole way to prevent any further accidental naps. Luckily, the ticket inspector took pity on me and didn't fine me for being the wrong side of Gatwick on a London–Gatwick ticket.

Finally I arrived at the airport at nearly 11.00 pm. Now all we had to do was make sure we didn't oversleep and miss our flight in the morning!

So, why Portugal?

The most common question people asked us before the move (and still ask us now) was, "So, why Portugal?"

We first visited Portugal not for cultural or intellectual reasons, but because we wanted a short holiday somewhere hot, cheap and only a quick flight away from London. It was off-season and we spent our days exploring magnificent beaches, taking cliff-top walks and swimming around curious rock formations in sheltered coves. Neither of us had expected to find so much natural, sun-kissed beauty so close to home. It was the start of our love affair with Portugal; and the more we came to know of the country, the more we wanted to live there.

In reality, there was a range of reasons for our move. First, we loved the food. Fresh sardines barbecued to perfection, clams swimming in buttery garlic sauce, rich duck rice, hot and spicy piri-piri chicken . . . We had always loved our food, and in Portugal it seemed we had found a country that cared about it as deeply as we did. Free time in England was often spent trying out new recipes and whole weekends were devoted to cooking and baking whenever we managed to escape the general chores associated with daily life. The prospect of preparing and eating so many new and delightful dishes appealed to both of us.

The cost of food in Portugal also drew us to the country.

A decent meal out in a restaurant could cost as little €15 per head. This included *couvert*, starter, main course, dessert, soft drink, wine, coffee and postprandial liqueurs. (*Couvert* is a kind of pre-starter provided in most Portuguese restaurants. It generally consists of bread, butter, sardine paste and olives, though each restaurant has its own version and additions, such as garlicky carrots or home-made tuna pâté.)

In London often just getting to and from the restaurant would cost us more than a whole meal in Portugal. The cost of wine was also a plus factor, with decent bottles costing around €2 in the supermarket and the really special ones costing €4.

We were also drawn to the Portuguese weather. The Algarve is reputed to have over 300 days of sunshine each year. With a seasonally affected husband who became gradually more grouchy as the long English winter months dragged by, this held a certain appeal.

The long and hot Portuguese summers attracted us because we love the sea. In England we headed to the coast as often as we could, but our plans were often thwarted by the traditional English summertime drizzle. In Portugal, we would have a choice of stunning beaches to explore all year round.

Frequent holidays in Portugal had given us a love of the Portuguese people and culture. In London the people we encountered in day-to-day life – shop staff, transport officials, etc. – were often surly and rude. In Portugal, we had always felt welcomed by the friendly and open nature of those we came into contact with. The focus of life was on family, food and relaxation, rather than on frenetic moneymaking and keeping up with the Joneses.

For me, if not so much for Ben, the language was another attraction. I've always loved learning languages and in school I had taken exams in French, German, Spanish and Latin. The idea of adding another language to my repertoire appealed, particularly one as challenging as Portuguese.

The combination of these different elements made an attractive package, but there was also something less tangible that had contributed to our final decision to emigrate. We had fallen in love with Portugal – we missed it when we were in England and eagerly planned our next break each time we returned from holiday. The setting sun making the sea turn pink, crumbling walls of ruined houses, bright flowers blooming on salt-lashed cliffs – all of these had somehow crept into our souls and made a part of us Portuguese without us even realising it was happening.

Arrivals

Since our original decision to emigrate, our lives had become a whirlwind of selling things, packing and saving every penny we could for our new life. I never would have believed how stressful it would be if anyone had told me. By the week before the move, I was getting about three or four hours' sleep a night, as the mixture of long working hours, excitement, panic at how much there was still to do and general nervousness combined to turn me into a hyperactive and stressed-out disaster. Thankfully, as we finally strolled around Gatwick before our flight, the months of stress and fretting seemed to just float away and I felt alive with excitement and anticipation. Suddenly it was all worth it – we were on our way.

Flying to Faro on one-way tickets to start our new life felt surreal. We were both excited on the flight and didn't speak much other than to keep repeating, "This feels so weird!" Months of planning and hard work had got us to this point and, now that it had arrived, neither of us could take it in.

After a brief tangle with the electronic passport gates upon arrival (Ben became trapped inside and had to be rescued by an immigration official) we stepped out of the airport into the welcoming warmth of the Portuguese sunshine.

We arrived in Tavira, our new home, half an hour later. After another ten minutes spent navigating the one-way system, we located the estate agent's office and went to sign our contract and collect the keys to our new home.

*

In order to validate our rental contract, we would need a fiscal number from the local *Finanças* – a council building providing all manner of useful financial services. In order to obtain a fiscal number, we needed proof of our address in Portugal. Thus, armed with our contract and pocket-size Portuguese dictionary, we headed to the *Finanças*, revelling in the brightness of the sun and the feel of the smooth cobbles beneath our feet. Beside us, the tidal river that runs through the centre of Tavira twinkled happily in the sunlight. Locals in huge wellington boots gathered clams while the seagulls circled noisily overhead.

In the *Finanças*, in nervous and stumbling Portuguese, I managed to express our desire for fiscal numbers to the lady behind the counter. She smiled and took our passports and contract. After photocopying them, she began tapping things into her computer. She frowned, turned to us and let out a stream of incomprehensible Portuguese.

Now, I had been learning Portuguese for months and could confidently order food at a market, ask for a table at a restaurant and exchange passing (if rather formal) pleasantries with strangers. I had also prepared for the particular nuances of the Algarve dialect, in which locals will drop as many syllables off the start and end of words as possible. I had been excited about practising speaking to actual people, rather than just replying to the woman on the CDs I had been learning from. For me, learning the language was a way of showing respect for my new countrymen. Speaking Portuguese is something that a surprising number of English expats in Portugal do not bother to do. I was determined not to be one of them.

Reality turned out to be rather more complicated than my CDs had prepared me for. The woman behind the counter saw my look of confusion, repeated her string of unintelligible words and handed back our passports with a shake of the head. There was no sign of fiscal numbers being produced. Ben had recognised the word "*banco*" so we surmised that payment was being demanded (it costs a few Euros to obtain a fiscal number). I tried handing over a €20 note. This resulted in a further avalanche of sound that we had no hope of understanding and the return of our €20. Going back to basics, I tried again:

"Please, I would like fiscal numbers for me and my husband."

"*Não é possível!*"

This I understood. In confusion, we left the *Finanças* and walked back to the rental agency, having failed to obtain the fiscal numbers required to validate our contract. The lovely English-speaking agent listened to our tale with surprise.

"Is not normal," she said, then provided us with our first example of what Ben and I have come to name "the Portuguese shrug".

The Portuguese shrug is one of the many expressive ways the Portuguese have of saying a huge amount without actually speaking. It can mean many things, including "I don't understand what the problem is," "This is unusual," "I cannot/will not help you," "What do you want me to do about it?" and "I really don't care." All without a single syllable being uttered.

The rental agent agreed to come back to the *Finanças* with us and act as translator. After a lengthy conversation with the lady behind the counter, she explained to us that we already had fiscal numbers. This was news to us. Apparently, when we opened our accounts a couple of months previously at the London branch of our Portuguese bank, the bank had needed fiscal numbers in order to complete the process. Unknown to us, the bank had given each of us a temporary / made up fiscal number. This did not appear to please the *Finanças*.

"Can't we just cancel those fiscal numbers and get new ones now?" I asked. (My naivety regarding Portuguese bureaucracy at that time was quite astounding.)

The rental agent explained that first our dodgy fiscal numbers would need to be removed from the system. This would take about three weeks. After that, we could come back to the *Finanças* and start again.

Thankfully, the rental agency was understanding of our situation and agreed to use our passport numbers as an interim measure to validate our contract. We were given the keys and set off through the streets of Tavira to go and inspect our new home.

The new house

It was months since we had viewed the property and we were both excited to see it again. It was exactly the kind of house we had pictured when we first talked about moving to Portugal – a traditional stone townhouse on a tiny cobbled street just wide enough for one car to drive down. The neighbouring properties were adorned with window boxes, filled with tumbling pink flowers, and washing lines flapping merrily in the sun. The loud bouncing of our suitcases over the cobblestones quickly attracted the attention of our new neighbours, who appeared in their doorways to observe our arrival.

Built in traditional Portuguese style, the house had stone walls and flagstone floors, which were perfect for keeping out the fierce summer heat. The living room and kitchen seemed smaller than we remembered, but the roof and ground floor terraces were larger, which fitted perfectly with our plans to spend as much time as possible outside in the sunshine. The roof terrace in particular excited us – it was large enough to accommodate a table, chairs, sun loungers and pot plants, and provided views across much of Tavira. Split across three floors, the house had three large bedrooms and two bathrooms – nearly twice the living space that we had had in London, and for less than half the price.

As the house was a holiday let that we had rented long term, it was already furnished and contained the essentials needed for daily life – which was good, as our own possessions were currently crossing the sea en route to Spain and not due to arrive in Portugal for another couple of days. It was a strange feeling – this was our home, yet it was filled with someone else's things. It didn't curb our enthusiasm though and we quickly set about unpacking our cases before venturing back into Tavira for lunch.

We wandered down the sun-dappled streets to the river, delighting in the warmth of the day and drinking in the sights and sounds of our new home. Palms and jacaranda trees lined the streets and flowers bloomed everywhere, with huge stands of birds of paradise (a particular favourite of mine) adorning the public gardens along the riverbank.

Crossing the river, we came across a tiny Portuguese take-away, bursting at the seams with locals chatting and laughing with the friendly owner. We decided to buy lunch there and take it back to eat on our roof terrace. We ordered piri-piri chicken, *arroz de pato* (duck rice), chips, rice, salad, four beers and two desserts. Ben wandered off at this point, leaving me at the till, panicking that the €30 clutched in my hand would not be enough to cover this feast. I needn't have worried; I had forgotten just how cheap good food is in Portugal – the bill came in at €11.

We retreated to our roof terrace to enjoy our lunch (which was delicious). The white buildings and orange rooftops of the town basked before us in the warm November sun, and we smiled as we ate, full of excitement and anticipation for the future.

After lunch, we found our local bar and sat outside drinking small Portuguese beers. The owner had no other customers, so came out to chat with us. Despite a rather stilted conversation (he spoke no English and our Portuguese was severely limited) we managed to explain that we had just moved in around the corner. He welcomed us happily and gave us our beers on the house. Although the ensuing silence was companionable enough, we determined to learn more Portuguese quickly so that we would be able to say something new to him each time we visited.

By bedtime, the fact that we lived in Portugal was still nowhere near sinking in. It felt more like we were on holiday – but a strange kind of holiday where we had to arrange things like Internet connections and mobile phones. It was a surreal feeling, but one that was accompanied by an enormous surge of happiness at being freed from London life and having the opportunity to live somewhere that was so special to both of us. We were excited to see what the future would hold.

Beaches and bureaucracy

Ben had extensively researched pretty much all aspects of life in Portugal – and particularly expat life in Portugal – before our move. The one thing that the research had flagged up again and again was the Portuguese love of paperwork and bureaucracy. It was this that had led us to sell our car in England, rather than trying to bring it with us, as the matriculation process was legendarily time consuming and expensive. Our first foray into the world of paperwork had been at the *Finanças* on the day we arrived and that had not gone well.

While we had been determined to enjoy at least a week off work after the move, we cracked after four days and decided we could survive no longer without an Internet connection, so headed into town to visit the local PT shop (the Portuguese equivalent of British Telecom). We needed to purchase mobile phones, a home phone, broadband and a TV package. Armed with our passports, tenancy agreement (as proof of address) and my trusty Portuguese–English dictionary, we felt well equipped to deal with the situation.

However, upon arrival at the PT shop we fell at the first hurdle. There was a ticket machine with three different options for tickets, depending upon the service you were there for.

The Portuguese love ticket machines. They use them in council offices, in the post office, in shops and even in some takeaways. In one of our local supermarkets, there is a ticket

machine with nearly 15 options, depending on which particular counter in the supermarket you wish to buy something
from.

This zealous use of ticket machines on every occasion
may seem a little strange, but I have come to understand it
as an effective way to combat another quirk of life here – the
Portuguese (at least in our town) seem to have no concept of
how to queue. In England you could open two tills in a shop
and customers would form two neat little lines of roughly the
same length, each person waiting patiently for their turn to be
served. In Portugal, this is an invitation to anarchy. A crowd
will form. People will jostle for position. Those not prepared
to assertively claim their right to service may well be there until the shop closes. Hence the use of ticket machines on every
possible occasion.

The ticket machine in the PT shop only had three options,
but we didn't know what any of them meant. We picked option B, waited for our number to come up, went to the counter and were promptly sent back to get a ticket for counter
A. There we were assisted by a lovely lady who thankfully
spoke enough English to make a sensible conversation possible when combined with our smattering of Portuguese. We
explained what we wanted.

"You have fiscal numbers?" was her first question. We
explained the problem with our fiscal numbers and that we
would not have them for another three weeks.

"*Não é possível.*" She shrugged.

I began to panic. I needed the Internet in order to work. If I
wasn't online within the next ten days, when my leave ended,
I would be in serious trouble. If I couldn't work from Portugal, I couldn't live in Portugal.

Luckily, Ben is often able to find practical solutions to
things rather than getting in a flap. He negotiated with the
PT lady and she agreed to use our passport numbers on the

paperwork, just as the rental agency had. In addition, he bought two plug-in dongles for our laptops, so we would have Internet access (albeit in a more expensive format) until the broadband had been arranged. After an hour in the PT shop (sadly, the first of many over the coming weeks), we left with pay-as-you-go mobiles and two dongles. Not quite what we had aimed to achieve, but a decent workaround that would enable us to communicate with the world and do our jobs. The Internet was scheduled for installation in three weeks' time – someone would phone us the day before the installation to confirm what time they would be turning up.

*

Satisfied that we had done all we needed to (or so we thought at the time), we relaxed and turned our attention to one of the more fun parts of our new life – beaches. Ben and I are both beach bums at heart. There is little we enjoy more than sitting on the sand and soaking up the sun, before charging full pelt into the sea to splash around like children in the waves. In England, any sunny weekend when we didn't have plans meant it was time to drive to a beach and enjoy the sea. Sadly, the occurrences of the sun shining at the weekend and us not having to work were few and far between.

Portugal's beaches were one of the key reasons we wanted to live here. The landscape from one end of the Algarve to the other varies dramatically. At the eastern end, where we had chosen to live, long sand-spit beaches hug the coast, providing miles of pale sand backed by the beautiful tranquillity of the Ria Formosa nature reserve. As you head further west, tall, crumbly cliffs in shades of deep yellow, orange and red lead down to tiny cove beaches and hidden grottos, many of them inaccessible by land, with rock formations dotted about in the sea adding to the natural wonder of this part of the country.

Although the western beaches are (arguably) more beautiful than those up "our" end of the Algarve, the eastern end is still a wonderful and very pretty place, which also tends to be a couple of degrees warmer than the west, both in air temperature and sea temperature.

As many of the beaches near us are sand-spit islands, most are accessed by boat, with local fishermen or larger ferry boats running tourists across to the beach for a few cents. Praia do Barril, to the west of Tavira, is slightly different in that access is via a tiny, narrow-gauge train that runs across the nature reserve straight to the sand. It is also possible to walk beside the tracks, which lead through marshes and lagoons before emerging from fragrant woodland onto the beach. Tiny crabs play in the shallows beside the tracks, while the sun dances and sparkles across the surface of the water.

Barril was one of the first beaches in our area that we visited after the move. It forms part of the Ilha de Tavira, which was recently listed as one of the top ten beaches in the world. As soon as we arrived we could see why. The sand was soft and powdery beneath our feet, like fine sugar, and had the whitish colour of the Caribbean. The sparkling sea stretched as far as we could see in both directions and low dunes provided shelter from the breeze, making it warm enough to sunbathe, despite it being November. As it was off-season, there was hardly anyone else around, just the owner of a small café serving ice-cold beer. It seemed we had found a hidden corner of paradise only ten minutes' drive from home.

On the way back from Barril we stopped in Santa Luzia, a rustic fishing village with a number of seafood restaurants. It is built along the river, on which small fishing boats bob merrily all day long. Determined to remain outside of our comfort zone and practise our Portuguese, we chose the shabbiest place we could find and stopped for a shellfish snack – a plate of large prawns, followed by cockles. The cockles were a revelation, served steaming hot in their shells, in a light sauce of coriander, garlic and olive oil. Every last cockle was devoured and the sauce mopped up with hunks of freshly baked bread. This simple concoction instantly became one of our favourite meals.

While we ate, I stared out at the fishing boats on the sparkling river. It seemed so strange that only a week ago we had been charging around London, desperately trying to get everything done before we moved. In this sleepy, sun-kissed village it felt as if time was standing still and I struggled to reconcile the pace of our previous life with this newfound peace and simplicity. I wondered how long it would be before I felt truly Portuguese, and when the hectic pace of London would be the bit that I found strange.

*

The following day, our explorations took us further east, towards the Spanish border. We arrived at Monte Gordo, which the guidebook had warned us would be a brash and over-touristy resort, full of high-rise buildings, burger joints and overpriced cocktail bars. Having grown up in Norfolk and regularly visited Great Yarmouth, this prospect filled me with eager curiosity rather than dread.

Monte Gordo was in reality everything the guidebook had promised but, with our childhood love of seaside places like Yarmouth, we were delighted. The beach was huge and much more sheltered and warm than the beaches immediately surrounding Tavira, and had it not been for the vast number of washed up jellyfish (and our lack of protective footwear) we might have been tempted to have a quick November swim. Monte Gordo beach also boasted views of Spain to the east, exciting us with the possibility of tapas dinners and road trips across mainland Europe.

Lunch was in a shabby-looking beach café on the sand.

We sat outside looking out to sea, marvelling that we were having to apply sun-cream in November. Lunch started well with a very pleasant meal of giant prawns and freshly grilled sole. Unfortunately it went downhill with the dessert, which had been sprinkled with cinnamon that tasted like it had been scraped from the back of a musty old wardrobe. The owner had been so nice we didn't have the heart to tell him, so we went and paid inside and beat a hasty retreat before he realised we hadn't eaten it. We ran across the sand, revelling in the joy of being on the beach in the sunshine.

On the way home we stopped to visit another beach – Praia Verde. Quite unusually for this part of Portugal, the beach is hidden by a large forest on the dunes, hence the name 'Green Beach'. Praia Verde was beautiful and completely deserted, which felt both romantic and slightly spooky. There wasn't a high-rise in sight and it seemed we had found another snap-shot of paradise within 15 minutes' drive of home. To have found such beautiful places within our first week, and so close to home, left both of us feeling excited about the days and weeks to come. What else would we discover as we ventured further afield?

Settling in

As November became December we began to feel settled in our new home. It still amazed us that we lived in Portugal – we would walk down the street and say to each other, "We live here!" Each new experience thrilled us, even if it was just finding a new *pastelaria* and trying one of their range of cakes – although we quickly learned we did not share the Portuguese love of putting candied egg yolk on many of their pastries! Each day seemed filled with excitement and opportunity, as well as the scary prospect of speaking our fledgling Portuguese in new situations.

We were, however, starting to establish a routine for our new life. I would put on a pot of coffee in the morning, then head to the local *pastelaria* at 8.00 am to buy a selection of pastries and chocolate milk. By the time I got back, the coffee would be ready and we would share breakfast before the day's work began.

Portuguese coffee is some of the best-tasting and strongest in the world, one of the benefits of Portugal's close links with South America. When accompanied by a sweet pastry, it is the perfect way to get the working day off to a good start. Many Portuguese reportedly also swear by a shot of brandy alongside their morning coffee, but I'm not sure my poor little English liver could manage that first thing in the morning.

Ben and I worked in separate rooms of the house. With

three bedrooms, we had plenty of room to each have our own work space – a far cry from our house in London, where the tiny spare bedroom had to double as a guestroom and office for both of us. In Portugal we spread out luxuriously to work, then reconvened for lunch, which we would enjoy on the roof terrace as often as the weather permitted.

December had brought with it some days of serious rain, which we delighted in. The strength of the downpours was like nothing we had experienced in England – going out in them meant being soaked through in a matter of seconds, no matter how many layers we were wearing. Being unused to such heavy rainstorms, we did once or twice go out in them deliberately just to experience their natural ferocity!

The frequency and violence of thunderstorms was also something we were not used to. As winter began in earnest, the distant rumble of thunder became something we listened out for, knowing it would soon be crashing directly over-head and making the windows rattle, while jagged bolts of lightning lit up the night sky. Often, the lights would dim or the television stop working, sometimes for a second, sometimes for several minutes. It was both invigorating and (for someone who's always been scared of the dark) a little frightening.

We still had some days of sunshine, which we made use of whenever possible, exploring Tavira and the surrounding area and gradually learning our way round our new home.

*

Proving that my remote working arrangement could be successful and add value to my company was important. Although I had occasionally worked from home when living in London, this was very different and did take some getting used to. It was strange to think of my colleagues, all sitting in the office together and sharing coffee and gossip in London, while I sat alone at my table in Portugal. There was an element of loneliness, but this was far outweighed by the joy of finding out simply how much work I was able to get through.

I've always loved being busy at work and am at my best when working on several projects simultaneously. I'm a hard worker and disapprove of slacking off in any form – I think "teacher's pet" sums it up nicely. I guess my attitude and commitment to work are partly why my company agreed to consider my unusual remote working proposal in the first place, so I make no apology for it!

With the usual office-based interruptions removed and the slight changes to my role that had been made in order for me to become a remote worker, my capacity to achieve things at work increased vastly. Projects that previously would have taken two or three weeks to complete were now taking me a week. My boss was delighted, as was I. I was able to achieve more, work more efficiently and still close my laptop and start my evening at five o'clock every day. The hell of the London commute was not something I missed.

*

The convenience of speaking in English to a phone company definitely *was* something I missed. The day before our broadband was due to be installed, we received a telephone call from PT:

"Hello, we are coming to install your broadband tomorrow, but first we need your fiscal number for the paperwork."

I explained that I did not have a fiscal number yet (I had been back to the town hall twice, but it was still "pending") and that in the PT shop they had used my husband's passport number on the paperwork.

Silence.

"Could you possibly use his passport number again?"

"*Não é possível.*" It may have been paranoia, but I felt certain I heard her shrug down the phone.

"So, what should we do about our broadband, please?"

"You have to wait until you have a fiscal number, then order it again."

And that was that – no flexibility, no negotiation, no broadband. We resigned ourselves to using pay-as-you-go our dongles for the foreseeable future.

*

The rain increased as December progressed, but conveniently abated for a few days while we received our first visitor from the UK – my dad. It was his first visit to Portugal and we were proud to show off our new home and new country. We toured the cobbled streets of Tavira and the sharply contrasting new shopping centre, ate fish from the barbecue at home and visited the beautiful beach at Ilha de Tavira.

This island beach is accessed via a small ferry running from the end of town. The beach has a campsite, a couple of small shops and a few restaurants. As it was early December there were few visitors and we had the beach mostly to ourselves. The weather was warm and although we didn't brave the water, the soft sand and the sun sparkling on the sea were very rewarding. After a pleasant while on the beach, we were hungry for lunch. There was only one restaurant open as it was off-season, so we settled in for a long, relaxed meal.

Unusually, there were no menus. We asked the waiter if the restaurant had cockles, but he said they did not. Instead he recommended a seafood stew, which we eagerly awaited while sipping icy-cold *vinho verde* ("green wine" – a fresh, slightly sparkling Portuguese wine made from very young grapes, which is the perfect accompaniment to fish). We were impressed when the stew arrived – a huge silver bowl filled with rice, prawns, clams and other seafood treats in a saliva-inducing red sauce.

Sadly, the first mouthful proved that our eyes and noses had deceived us. The clams were gritty with sand from not having been cleaned thoroughly and the fish was dry almost to the point of chewiness. We persevered, hoping to find some more delectable morsels below the surface, but gave up half-way through, deciding instead that next time we visited Ilha de Tavria we would bring a picnic. It was (and still remains) the only truly bad meal we have eaten in Portugal since we moved here. Although disappointed, we saw the funny side and it provided a happy, if unusual, memory of my dad's first visit to a Portuguese beach.

It was while my dad was staying that I experienced my first true victory in terms of tackling the language – a conversation with our neighbour. Although we had managed simple transactions in shops and ordered food in restaurants, this was the first time that I had managed a Portuguese conversation in a social setting. I say "managed" – in reality the poor woman must have felt like she was conversing with a four-year-old. Nevertheless, I managed to answer her questions (the usual pleasantries – Where are you from? Do you have any children?), when she stopped for a chat as I was taking the rubbish out. Too nervous to ask her any questions in return, I was nevertheless elated with my success and rushed back into the house to tell Ben and my father all about it. I relayed my victory over a glass of wine, before sheepishly heading back out to retrieve and bin the sack of rubbish – which in my excitement I had left lying in the middle of the street.

Unfortunately, our next interaction with the same neighbour was not quite so successful!

The monster

When we moved to Portugal, I had been prepared for (although not happy about) the increased number of insects. Flies and wasps abounded over the summer months and I had accepted that weird looking spiders and dreaded cockroaches would inevitably become a part of our life. What I had not been expecting were the giant crickets.

On holidays to Portugal, Ben and I had often delighted in dining as dusk fell and listening to the gentle whirr of crickets in the long grass gradually rise in a frenzied crescendo. I had imagined innumerable tiny crickets happily going about their crickety business.

When we first moved into our house, I noticed a cricket on the kitchen window's shutters, in the little walled terrace area at the back. It was longer than my hand (*Husband's note: no, it wasn't*), browny-grey and looked like something out of my nightmares. It seemed to be hibernating so I did my best to ignore it (although I kept a close eye on it each time I had to hang out the washing). A week passed without the cricket moving and I had begun to relax a little about its presence, when suddenly one morning I went outside to find it had re-positioned itself. It was now resting snugly in a patch of sun on the kitchen windowsill. Despite my anxiety at this new development, I continued in my attempts to live in harmony with nature by leaving it be.

Two days later, I went outside and saw that the cricket had gone. Delighted, I turned back to the kitchen door to fetch the basket of washing I had intended to hang out. My hand was halfway to the door when I saw it – sitting by the door handle and flexing its enormous legs. I panicked and fled into the house, slamming the door behind me.

Had it been a smaller cricket, I would have just put a glass over it, slid a piece of paper underneath and released it into the street at the front of the house, freeing it to roam the town at will. However, given the size of this cricket, a glass simply wouldn't be big enough. Even our glass jug was not big enough.

I took a photograph and consulted friends online. Their resounding advice was to kill it. Not only did I not have the stomach for this, I also wasn't entirely sure who would win in a battle to the death – me or the cricket. I was bigger (just) but the cricket had wings, could move a lot faster than me and wasn't utterly terrified.

After some minutes of sitting indoors and stewing about what was to be done, I came up with a plan. I found our largest Tupperware container and crept outside, ready to put it over the cricket and then slide the lid under, neatly trapping it. However, my fear mastered me – I couldn't bring myself to get close enough to the cricket to put the tub over it. Shamefaced, I retreated inside once more. Determined not to be defeated, I improvised with a squeegee floor mop and some strong parcel tape, producing a Tupperware tub on the end of a long pole. Now I was ready!

Advancing outside once more and emboldened by my ability to keep a good distance away from the cricket, I made my move. And missed. The cricket leapt in panic at my misjudged thrust with the Tupperware and shot past me (I shrieked and jumped backwards into the washing line). It settled at the other end of the little terrace and we watched each other warily. I tried again but the cricket jumped further away before I got near. My third attempt was successful and my improvised cricket trap worked – the furious creature was now trapped on the floor inside the container.

I slid my way along the mop pole and after a minute or so of maneuvring managed to get the lid under the tub. Success! Calling Ben down from his work to come and open the front door for me, I emerged into the street to release the monster. Our neighbours were outside chatting. They broke off their conversation and stared in surprise when they saw me emerge with my mop/Tupperware contraption. Trying to act casual, I placed the box on the street and unclipped the lid, sliding it out from underneath before shaking the container to release the cricket and dashing back inside the house.

Unfortunately the cricket shot out of the tub and promptly landed on the friendly neighbour's stomach. Peeping out of the door, I saw her look down and then casually flick it away, her face full of amusement at the antics of the silly English girl across the road. Thankfully, she didn't hold the fact of me throwing a giant monster cricket at her against me and over the following weeks our stilted but amiable conversations continued.

(The cricket saga was actually not over. Having escaped the back of the house, it settled in for a nice long stay on our front door. It remained there for nearly two weeks, during which time I squeaked in fright every time I entered or exited the house. Finally, after a few too many glasses of wine with dinner at a local restaurant, Ben took matters into his own hands and swiped the cricket off the door before chasing it down the street. It fled and I was finally safe once more.)

The rain

When my dad went home at the end of his week with us in mid-December, he took the sunshine with him. It began to rain as I drove back from the airport. Being from England I don't mind a bit of rain – I'm used to it. The rainy weather meant that we could enjoy some traditional English meals that it had thus far felt too hot to eat, such as beef stew and dumplings.

There are limits though. During that first winter in the Algarve, it began to rain in mid-December and did not stop until mid-February. It was the wettest Portuguese winter since records began in 1870. Our traditional stone townhouse was freezing. Without central heating, we relied on reverse cycle air conditioning and oil-filled radiators to try and keep out the chill, but to no avail. The house stubbornly refused to warm up, despite our rocketing electricity bills.

Dressing in the morning now involved thick tights, jeans, woolly socks over the tights and at least three layers of jumpers. And we were still cold. This was not what we had envisaged when dreaming of our new life in the sun.

As the rain continued, the situation in our house deteriorated. The windows leaked. The doors leaked. Puddles of rainwater gathered in every room and mould began to appear – black mould on the walls and ceilings, green mould on our wooden furniture and white mould on the floor tiles. We spent hours mopping up rainwater, bleaching walls and vainly attempting to dehumidify the house. Nothing worked, and despite our best efforts the mould spread. We consulted the letting agency. After much regretful shaking of the head and muttering of "Is not normal," they agreed to send their cleaners round to tackle the mould. The cleaners did a tremendous job and with their professional tools were able to reach the mould on the high ceilings, which I had been unable to do. The house smelt so strongly of bleach when they had finished that my throat was raw, but we were finally mould free!

The other problem the rain had caused was a lack of clean clothes; or more specifically a lack of dry clothes. We didn't have a tumble dryer or central heating (gone were the English winter days of drying clothes on radiators) so had to rely on hanging things on the washing line outside. Outside – where it was raining almost non-stop. I was lucky if I could get one load of clothes washed and dried in a week. Given the large number of items we were wearing to try and keep warm, not to mention the towels we were using to mop up all the rain that was getting into the house, the situation quickly became ridiculous. Piles of dirty washing filled one of our spare bedrooms. Wet towels waiting to be washed began to moulder. Every morning when I got up, instead of putting on the coffee and going out for pastries, my first task was now to grab that day's soggy underwear from the washing line and dry it with my hairdryer. Somehow it did not feel quite like we were living the dream life in the sun that we had envisaged!

Echoes of England

The one thing we had been determined not to do when we moved to Portugal was to join the expat community in the English bars. We wanted to be part of the Portuguese community, not the English one; that was part of the reason we had moved to Portugal. However, after weeks of battling with bureaucracy and ridiculous rain, we realised that we had both begun to miss the sound of English voices around us. There was an English bar close to our house and, although we had pointedly ignored it since our arrival, it suddenly seemed the epitome of cosiness and safety. We took the plunge and headed through the doors.

We were greeted by a friendly, cheerful English lady, who we talked with non-stop for the next four hours, sharing our trials and tribulations over several small glasses of ice-cold beer. We returned home at the end of the evening rather surprised at having enjoyed ourselves so much in the dreaded expat bar.

Over the next few weeks we became regulars in the bar and developed a friendship with the landlady. The struggling world economy had had its impact on Portugal and on her business, so the three of us spent many hours coming up with plans and schemes in order to boost customer numbers and sales. One such plan was to host a local book club, which was in the process of being set up.

Book club started well. Local expats turned up to the first meeting and discussed their tastes in reading. Although these were wide-ranging (including one gentleman who announced, "I don't read fiction"), we managed to agree on a book that everyone was willing to read over the coming month. Only the non-fiction man seemed unimpressed with the choice. The group lingered in the bar for drinks after book club was over: the night was a success.

Sadly subsequent meetings did not go so well. After two drunken incidents at consecutive meetings, including one where a regular of the bar reviewed at great length a book which nobody else had read – while swearing prolifically about that month's chosen literary offering – book club was disbanded.

There were other memorable nights in the bar. It was there that I first tasted *medronho*. *Medronho* is a kind of fruit brandy, made with fruit from the strawberry tree. It's a very traditional drink and is apparently sometimes drunk for breakfast by the Portuguese people in order to fortify them for the day ahead.

Having been told all of this by a local in the bar, I figured it couldn't be too bad – if Portuguese housewives could drink *medronho* for breakfast before completing their daily chores, then surely a few sips after work couldn't harm me. Or so I assumed.

After only one glass of the evil liquor, I became extremely merry. My memories of the rest of the evening are a little blurred. I recall having a lengthy conversation with a local railway worker about a set of teeth he was having custom made for him from the teeth of a crocodile. At least I think that's what he said. Although the *medronho* had convinced me I could speak fluent Portuguese, I suspect that actually that was not the case and that there may have been some crossed wires during the conversation.

As well as having crocodile teeth, the gentleman was

famous locally for his one-man brass section act. As the evening passed, he showed us his uncanny ability to play the trumpet, trombone and tuba – all without an instrument in sight.

The next thing I knew, it was morning. I woke up on the sofa with a pounding headache and no recollection of why I wasn't in bed. I felt desperately sick and the daylight seemed to burn through my eyes and directly into my brain. I vowed never to drink *medronho* again – a vow which, to this day, I have kept.

The festive season

A few days before Christmas, on a rare Saturday when the rain held off for a few hours and the sun came out, we went for a drive further west along the Algarve, to check out some of the little cove beaches around Carvoeiro. Advised by the guidebooks to avoid these areas during high season, this was the perfect time of year to visit. With no crowds, the incredible natural beauty (that leads to these beaches becoming overrun by tourists during the summer months) can be truly appreciated.

The first stop on our tour was Benagil – a small cove beach backed by stunning cliffs. The sun was sparkling on the sea and, with the cliffs protecting the beach from the wind, a few hardy souls were even sun-bathing, despite it being mid-December.

After stopping at a little beachfront café for a beer in the sunshine, we drove on to Praia da Marinha. This was another sheltered cove beach, surrounded by huge cliffs and interesting rock formations. We wandered eastward along the clifftops, admiring the resilient, salt-loving flowers and plants as we walked. The sea twinkled to our right, the ever-shifting shades of blue and green making a beautiful setting for the occasional sailboat that drifted across it. Upon returning to the car, we noticed a map showing scuba diving and snorkelling routes around the bay, which promised a close-up encounter with the sea-creatures inhabiting the waters of this part of the world. Although not something we did that day (the sea really was too chilly by December), this went on the list of things to do the following summer.

After our cliff-top meander, we headed into Guia, near Albufeira, for some retail therapy in the substantial Algarve Shopping complex. It was hugely busy (unsurprising given that Christmas was so close) and so after just a quick look round we decided to head home, despite the lure of the tinsel and baubles everywhere.

On the way back to the car park, my poor husband encountered his greatest fear – a large, black rodent ran across the pavement right in front of us. Bolting back to the car, he vowed never to return to Algarve Shopping! However, the stunning red, purple and orange sunset that we were treated to as we drove home – followed by a beer when we arrived – served to calm his nerves eventually.

*

In the midst of all our mould disasters came our first Portuguese Christmas. I have to confess – I adore Christmas. From the start of October onwards, I nag my Ben to let me play Christmas carols in the house 24/7. By mid-October I will be looking through recipe books and making lists of all the things I want to cook (well, ask Ben to cook – he is the chef of the family). The opening of the Christmas box, which contains all of our tinsel, baubles and other festive bits and pieces, is always an exciting time for me. So is the putting up of the tree on 1 December, when I am free to dash around the house putting tinsel and twinkly lights everywhere I can reach.

If he's honest, Ben gets almost as excited as me about Christmas. We had both been concerned that the festive season in Portugal, so far away from our family, friends and usual English traditions, wouldn't feel right. We had worried that Christmas in a country where you couldn't easily buy mince pies or brandy butter just wouldn't feel the same.

Our worries were quickly dispersed. The Portuguese seem to love Christmas – perhaps even more than the English do. They have two bank holidays in early December, which definitely helps to get everyone in the mood.

As December approached, lights and decorations appeared everywhere. Tavira at night became a winter wonderland, with lights strung along the river banks and throughout the town. The town square became home to a huge Christmas tree, while a magical, trumpet-blowing angel made of thousands of tiny lights appeared in the bandstand. To add to the atmosphere, outdoor speakers were placed strategically around the town, piping out cheering Christmas music wherever we went. For me, this was Christmassy perfection.

With an 84.5% Roman Catholic population, the religious aspects of Christmas are more widely appreciated in Portugal than in the UK. Nativity scenes sprang up everywhere – both in shops and as part of the town decorations. We bought a little candle-lit one, along with various boxes of lights and baubles, which proudly joined our English decorations and transformed our house into something akin to Santa's grotto.

The lack of mince pies turned out not to be an issue. Our regular work trips to England meant we were able to source everything we needed to make our own, which turned out to be much nicer than anything shop-bought. Our home-made brandy butter was also a success. The increased use of the oven also went some way towards combating the bone-chilling cold of our house!

*

We had worried that spending Christmas on our own in Portugal, while all our family and friends were in the UK, would feel a little flat. However, the festive atmosphere that surrounded the town, combined with the fact that on 22nd December we finally received our fiscal numbers from the *Finanças*, meant that we were just as excited as if we had been in England. Despite the fact that an important project meant I had to work up until late on Christmas Eve, we still had plenty of time during December to wrap our gifts, try out a variety of festive Portuguese culinary delights and buy our turkey for Christmas lunch.

The gift-shopping was particularly fun. We were used to shopping centres in London – filled with shouting teenagers and bad-tempered queues in Primark. In Portugal things were very different. As well as the usual sort of shops we expected, shopping centres tended to include a decent, paved area with cafés and fountains, a cinema and a large food court combining Portuguese fast-food with the inescapable American favourites. It was common to see three or four generations of a Portuguese family out shopping together, the whole experience providing a family day out.

This was a new concept to me – in London shopping centres were something to rush in and out of in as little time as possible. However, as we sat under the lights of the impressive Christmas tree, drinking Portuguese espresso at 60 cents a cup (me) and glasses of beer at 90 cents (Ben), we did start to see the fun that could be had whilst shopping in Portugal. The fact that parking for shopping centres in Portugal is free meant that we could linger over our drinks without fear of racking up London-style parking charges. Even Ben admitted that he was enjoying himself – most unusual given that we had already been in the shopping centre for over two hours (I think the beer helped).

We ended up staying over four hours to purchase our main

load of Christmas gifts, with regular refreshment breaks complementing the shopping. This was a breakthrough – in London, Christmas shopping was invariably stressful and would end with cross words and frayed tempers. In Portugal, we had spent longer in the shopping centre than we had intended, bought everything we needed and actually had fun in the process.

With arms full of bags, we headed back home to wrap everything before the arrival of the big day.

Christmas!

Christmas day arrived and the moment came to cook our enormous turkey. As with most joints of meat you buy in the supermarket here, it came without cooking instructions, so the Internet and a good oven thermometer were already on hand. The real problem came when we opened up the turkey's packaging – and found it still had a neck. And some guts.

Ben bravely set to work. Sadly our kitchen knives were not as sharp as they could have been and a messy, bloody half hour of sawing and hacking followed. Not quite the champagne and gift opening that we had visualised for our first Christmas morning in Portugal!

I used to be quite squeamish when it came to butchering meat and before we moved to Portugal would certainly never have pictured myself happily gutting fish and removing animals' necks. Out of necessity that soon changed and as well as honing my butchery skills, I gained a new-found respect for the strength of Portuguese housewives' stomachs.

By Christmas night we were suitably full of food and drink and had exchanged our gifts, spoken to our nearest and dearest and had a thoroughly enjoyable day. We had indulged in an English-style Christmas lunch with all the trimmings (albeit with a sad lack of parsnips, which were not to be found in our part of Portugal). Although we both moved to Portugal with a view to becoming more Portuguese – speaking the language, learning cultural traditions and so forth – it turned out that Christmas lunch was something we were not prepared to compromise on. I guess however long we live here there will always be parts of us that are stubbornly English – and Christmas tradition seems like it will be one of them.

When New Year's Eve arrived, we were determined to celebrate in Portuguese style. Despite both being quite unwell (a combination of mould-related illnesses and over-indulgence in rich food and wine), we copied our neighbours and ascended to our roof terrace with a bottle of Portuguese bubbly (we splashed out and paid €7 for the really good stuff) to listen to the live music drifting towards us from the centre of town and to watch the fireworks.

The Portuguese love firework displays and turn out to see them in large numbers – perhaps because the sale of fireworks to individuals without licences is not something which is permitted, so formal displays are the only chance to see them. Several times a year, national holidays are a cause for celebration with live music and huge pyrotechnic displays – and New Year's Eve is the biggest of them all. Tavira's show was truly breathtaking. Lasting about 20 minutes, it was set intricately to music and was more impressive than any of the fireworks shows we had been to in London – not bad for a quaint little fishing town with only 20,000 inhabitants.

On New Year's Day we both felt a little better and ventured out into Tavira's main square in the evening, where the New Year celebrations were still going on, with a band playing rock cover-versions in a temporary arena. We wandered around, soaking up the atmosphere and drinking ridiculously cheap beer from the little stalls that had popped up around the square. It was nearly midnight, but children were still running around and dancing and the atmosphere was one of cheerful celebration. I commented that an event like this would not be possible in London without crowds of police and security guards there to control the fun.

Moments after this remark, a large explosion came from about three feet behind where we were standing at the back of the crowd watching the band. I screamed and we both leapt forward. Those around us scattered and the band stopped playing mid-song. It turned out that a firework had been thrown at the crowd by someone on the bridge. Large scorch marks could be seen on the marble tile at our feet. Had it landed any closer, it would have done us serious harm – it wasn't just a little firecracker.

Our ears were ringing and we were both shaken up. It was a horrible moment, as my Portuguese deserted me and I could only stare mutely at the people in the crowd asking what had happened. The singer on the stage was shouting in Portuguese, but all I caught was the word for "idiot".

One of the men in the crowd saw the scorch marks on the marble-tiled ground and called angrily to his companions. There was much muttering and shaking of heads as they examined the spot. One of them spoke to us, but we couldn't understand his question. Instead Ben just pointed across the bridge to where the firework had been thrown from.

That was enough – the man and his friends spotted the perpetrator and suddenly about 30 of them bolted across the bridge, only to return empty-handed a minute or two later. I was disappointed that the firework-thrower had escaped punishment, although a beating by 30 drunk, angry men was also not something I would have liked to witness.

We left shortly afterwards and as we walked home I kept looking over my shoulder – something I had not felt the need to do since I used to walk home from work in the dark in London. Gradually my fear began to turn to anger, with a little paranoia thrown in for good measure. We were the only English people in the crowd – had the firework been thrown aimlessly or had we been singled out because we weren't

Portuguese? A nasty thought, but one I couldn't quite shake off.

We were both glad to be safely back inside our house and a stiff drink helped to calm our nerves. Ben was as angry as I was by now – whether a stupid prank or a purposeful attack, the reality was that we had been only a few feet away from ending up in hospital. We were too hyped up to even think of sleep, so scoured Facebook to see if any of our friends in England were still awake. They were, and thus the very first of our impromptu Skype parties – which soon became something of a legend – was born.

We knew it would be easy to lose touch with people once we moved abroad. Coming from an active social circle, we were worried that we would miss the nights out, the weekend barbecues and the million and one other things we did with our friends in London. We were also realistic enough to realise that some friends-of-friends, who we used to bump into on the periphery of our social circle, might disappear altogether.

As it turned out, the loneliness we had anticipated did not materialise – we were happy in each other's company and life was full of exciting new discoveries as we explored our new country and its customs. Additionally, our Skype call packages meant that for about £4.50 per month we could call any landline in England for free, so long calls to friends and family meant we stayed in touch.

Facebook also kept us up to date with the goings-on of our friends and we delighted in seeing regular photographs and video clips of what everyone was up to. We also posted our own pictures, meaning that our new life (including the infamous monster cricket saga) was shared with all those near and dear to us.

Our first Skype party was a revelation. Having seen that some friends were still awake and online after our near miss with the firework, we video-called London, where it turned out that a few of our closest friends were having post-pub drinks at one of their houses. We relayed the evening's events to them, along with our worries that we had been singled out because we were foreigners. They quickly told us not to be so daft and advised us to have a drink with them. We were happy to oblige.

We suggested a round of shots and as they didn't have any shot glasses, they improvised with egg cups. We happened to have matching ones, so we filled those and all chinked our egg cup 'glasses' to the camera. For the next couple of hours we took it in turns to play songs to each other and danced and drank the night away as though we were all together. The negative feelings of the firework incident were swept away and a lovely evening was had by all – proving that we didn't need to be in the same country to keep in touch and have a good night in with our friends.

A new year

By January we had lived in our new country for two months. Many things still felt strange, but it was amazing how many simple triumphs could be achieved in one week, such as successfully exchanging our empty gas bottle for a new one, being remembered and welcomed in a restaurant, and successfully utilising a few newly learned words. We were discovering that the smallest things could make settling in a new country feel so much easier.

We were also taking time to explore our new surroundings. The massive Ria Formosa natural park spreads eastwards from Faro, past Tavira and on towards Spain. Dotted with salt pans, where in places salt is still harvested without machines in the traditional way, this wide expanse of land is teeming with wildlife and fascinating to explore. As it joins tidal inlets in several places, it hosts a number of ever-changing seascapes.

The inlet between Ilha de Tavira and the mainland swiftly became one of our favourite haunts. After a hard day at work, a good, leg-stretching walk to this part of our local area never failed to relax us. On each visit the scenery would be different, with little bits of beach and rock accessible or submerged depending on the tides. Fishermen would dot the landscape, sometimes in small clusters on the shore and at other times on their own in boats moored in the channel.

The area also had its own ruined fort and we spent several happy hours climbing over the ruins and looking at the scenery (Ben) or pretending to fight off historical invaders (me). It was only after some weeks that we realised the name of the fort (Forte de Rato) meant "Fort of the Mouse". Ben's rodent phobia meant that our visits to the area were restricted to the beach thereafter.

Although spurned as a beach by the Portuguese (they have so many more beautiful ones to choose from), the charm of this little inlet captured our hearts – going there became one of those free, life-affirming activities that we had dreamed of finding when we pictured ourselves living in Portugal.

*

As January rolled into February our efforts to learn Portuguese came on slowly but surely. We would go to the supermarket and realise that we knew the names of more items each time. I was able to write the shopping list (well, most of it) in Portuguese. However, conjugating verbs and constructing full sentences remained something of a mystery. To combat this, I purchased a great big book called *501 Portuguese Verbs*.

Having always loved learning languages, I read the introduction with eager anticipation. The prognosis was not good. All it taught me was that it would be at least a decade before I could become anything approaching fluent. Having completed the introduction, I put the book on our coffee table, where it remained untouched for weeks to come, silently taunting me with the horrific complexity of this beautiful language.

When I was a child, a French colleague of my father who had been living in England for many years told me that you know you have truly become part of your new country when you think and dream in that language. Other than the odd word, I was definitely still thinking in English. And apart from one dream in which I was trying to speak Portuguese and getting the words wrong, I was still dreaming in English too. Still, it had only been a few months and I was determined to keep practising. I pinned another easy word-list to the fridge and studiously ignored the verb book.

*

Our explorations took us a little further afield in early February, when a sunny weekend, combined with the fact that we had hired a car for a couple of weeks, allowed us to explore more of the beaches along the central part of the Algarve coastline. Our first stop was Santa Eulália, a popular spot backed by the trademark orange cliffs. After a quick drink, we went for a long walk along the beach, climbing over rocks and through sparkly rock-pools to reach the quiet coves past the headland. A few people (braver than us) splashed in the sea, but we ignored the cold February waters and continued our tour to Olhos de Agua.

Despite a recommendation we had read online, this was a major disappointment – English bars, cafés and restaurants with menus entirely in English, and English football playing on big screens in almost every venue. This was the exact opposite of what we had moved to Portugal for. We moved swiftly on, detouring into the tourist hellhole that is Albufeira for a quick snack as our hunger couldn't wait for the next beach. We found ourselves surrounded by English tourists ordering food and drink without even attempting to say please or thank you in Portuguese, something which I find particularly rude. Again, we quickly moved on.

A little further to the west, we found ourselves at the less well-known beach of Praia dos Três Irmãos, a fairytale beach between the busy resorts of Praia da Rocha and Alvor, which we had discovered during a cliff-top walk on a holiday some five years previously. We first came across it after rambling over the cliffs and coming quite unexpectedly across a dark corridor leading to a lift. Curious at finding a lift built into the cliff, we had taken it to see where it went and had emerged into a tiny bar/restaurant looking out over a gorgeous sunny cove. We had spent several happy hours there, eating piping hot sardines before splashing into the rolling waves. The whole place had a real air of being a secret beach and we were keen to find it again, having had such a lovely afternoon there on our previous visit.

We set off on foot from Alvor and after a lengthy walk along the sand, feet splashing in the chilly sea, we spotted a familiar-looking cliff and scrambled up it, convinced our fairytale beach would be on the other side. Halfway up the cliff, we found the lift – or at least we found a wooden panel blocking an entranceway where we were sure the lift had been previously. Assuming the place must be closed for winter, we carried on upwards until we found a gap in the rocks and were able to peer down. And there it was – what was left of the restaurant.

Whether by falling rocks or bad weather or some other factor, the place had been destroyed. We had waited years to find it again and now that we had, it was nothing but a ruin. Always glass-half-full, we were still delighted to have found the beach we remembered so fondly, even if the lack of lift and the tide being in meant that we couldn't actually set foot on it. We returned home happy after our day of adventuring. Sadly, neither of us anticipated that we would once more be returning to the house of mould.

Mould 2: return of the killer mould

Despite a couple of mould-free weeks around Christmas, our disasters were not over. As the rain continued into February, the mould came back with a vengeance. We noticed a few spots in the bathroom, then the bedroom. We moved into another bedroom while we bleached the first one. The mould followed us. It crept into every nook and cranny. Our clothes began going mouldy in the wardrobes. Spare pillows and duvets became covered in it. Our lovely little terracotta dishes in the kitchen came out of the cupboards with green fur on them. We developed coughs, sore throats and earache. Still we battled on – scrubbing everything in sight each night with bleach when we finished work and tackling the high ceilings as best we could at the weekends.

One rainy Friday evening in early February we decided to play a board game. It was a rare game that I had managed to track down for Ben's birthday a few years ago, as he had enjoyed playing it in his childhood. I pulled it off the shelf and found that the box was mouldy. I opened it up and found that inside the paper money had started to crinkle from the damp. It was the last straw.

In a temper I began to examine our possessions – every last one of them. I pulled our books off the shelves and found that at least half of them were covered in mould. I discovered that Ben's wedding suit was mouldy. The flowers that my mother had dried from our wedding were mouldy and had to be thrown away. The mattress in one of the bedrooms had gone green. The carved wooden fish mobile that Ben had bought me for Christmas some years ago was white and furry. I moved the fridge and found a damp, mouldering patch that spread halfway up the wall, with chunks of paint flaking off. I moved the bookcase and found a two-metre tall patch of black mould sitting behind it.

Enough was enough. The next morning I went back to the letting agency. My anger of the night before had subsided and instead I was close to tears as I told them about the state of the house. They promised to send the cleaners back.

The cleaners were horrified. Having dealt with a large number of mould problems over the past six weeks – the whole Algarve was beset by it due to the rains and the lack of damp proof coursing in Portuguese buildings – they said that our house was the worst property they had seen. We reported this back to the rental agency and asked to move – we couldn't stand it any more. Having only taken the tenancy for six months originally, we had already lined up our next property through the same agency (a modern, mould-free apartment in a nearby village), so we asked to move in there early.

The agency said it couldn't be done – we could not break our current contract without risking being sued by the landlord. They seemed set on not helping us, so we took matters into our own hands and spoke to a man from another agency. He showed us round a couple of flats, one of which we instantly fell for. It had even more space than our house, as well as a built-in barbecue on one of the balconies and a split-level roof terrace. We were taking a final tour before signing on the dotted line (intending to deal with the consequences of having to pay rent for two properties later) when Ben noticed a few tiny black specks on the wall in the master bedroom.

"What's this?" he queried.

"Oh, just a bit of mould – I'm sure it won't be a problem."

In despair we abandoned the flat and headed to a local bar to drown our sorrows. I checked my email quickly on the bar's computer. I had a message from the rental agency saying that our current landlord was prepared to let us break the contract early – at the end of February – and that we could move into the new flat on 1st March. I quickly emailed them an acceptance and our sorrow-drowning became a celebration which lasted long into the night.

It was only the next morning when, somewhat the worse for wear, we realised that it was 27th February – we had to move house in two days' time.

The following days were a ridiculous whirlwind of packing, cleaning and organising. Somehow we managed it and on 1st March moved into our new, mould-free apartment, ready for a drama-free life.

Sadly, our new-found peace lasted less than 24 hours.

A fresh start

Our new apartment was in a sleepy little village, which linked to a marginally larger village just over the railway tracks. The two villages are a strange mixture of the old and the new. One used to be a tiny collection of fishermen's huts, dotted along the beautiful scenery of the tidal river, with sand dunes on the other side and the sea beyond. Tourism has led to the villages' expansion, until the two have essentially merged into one large village, although they have retained their separate names. Thus apartment building complexes with swimming pools have sprung up around the traditional properties. Off-season, the villages retain a great deal of their original charm. During the summer months the same cannot be said, but the atmosphere is always one of sunshine and beach-based fun, which suits us perfectly.

Our apartment was the absolute opposite of what we wanted before we moved to Portugal. Instead of a traditional house on a cobbled street, it was a new-build apartment in a block. We loved it from the moment we moved in. It had two large balconies, which due to the building's design gave us covered areas as well as open space, meaning we could still be outside (and dry washing!) when it rained.

The way the apartment faced meant that we had sun on the back balcony in the morning and on the front one in the afternoon – so we always had the option to sit in the sun or the shade, no matter what time of day it was. Inside, the apartment was spacious yet somehow cosy at the same time. It was also tastefully decorated and entirely mould-free. Of the six apartments in our block, ours was the only one with tenants, so we could make as much noise as we wanted without having to worry about the neighbours. To top it all off, the apartment complex also had a pool. It was the perfect setting for a quiet, peaceful home.

However, just as we had moved the last of our boxes into the new apartment, one of the ladies from the rental agency arrived at the door with a camera. After some arm-waving and frantic signalling to help overcome the language barrier, it transpired that she wanted to take a photograph of one of our sofa cushions. Perplexed, we examined the cushion closely – and noticed the large bottom-shaped print that she had evidently come to take a picture of.

We phoned the agency and spoke to one of the English-speaking staff. She asked if we had been in the apartment that morning and left wet towels on the floor, as the cleaners had found them when they did their final checks before we moved in. I confirmed that we had not. The agency then informed us that someone unknown to them must have a key to our flat. They said that this was very common with new-build apartment blocks, due to the number of people who would have been working on it while it was built. They surmised that one of the builders must have used the pool and then used our apartment to shower and dry in.

So it transpired we had moved all of our things into an apartment to which a stranger had a key. Suddenly the emptiness of the block did not quite seem like such a good thing. With the usual laid-back Portuguese attitude, the agency said they would organise a locksmith to change the lock and issue us with new keys in a few days' time.

"A few days' time? But that means a stranger could walk

into our home at any moment! And what if we go out? They could come in and take whatever they wanted! We've only been here for a couple of hours and haven't changed the contents insurance to this address yet!"

"Oh, I'm sure you won't be burgled."

This was not reassuring. After some debate, we managed to arrange that the locksmith would come the following day.

After hurriedly changing the address on our contents insurance, we settled down (with a baseball bat under the bed just in case) for our first night's sleep in our new home. After an hour of tossing and turning anxiously, we got up and went onto the balcony to smoke a cigarette. It was from there that we spied a man dressed in black prowling around the neighbourhood. Not really what you want to see at 1.00 am when you know that somebody out there has the key to your front door. We watched him wander from our road and disappear down the adjoining one. Ten minutes later he was back. And so began a night of obsessively staring off both balconies, trying to keep tabs on the prowler. It continued until 4.30 am when exhaustion finally overcame fear and we managed to get a few hours of sleep.

The next morning I phoned the agency to check when the locksmith would arrive. I reported the prowler to them. They informed me that he was a security guard, employed to patrol the area at night until more of the apartments were occupied. Feeling stupid, I thanked them and waited for the arrival of the locksmith.

*

About a week after moving into the apartment, a man buzzed on the intercom, saying he was from EDP (our electricity company). I let him in the block door and waited for him to come upstairs to read our meter. When he didn't appear after a minute or so, I went downstairs to find him. He had already left – all that remained was a printed letter in the block's main electricity cupboard. After a quick translation, with a little help from Google, we established that the note read something along the lines of: "As the electricity bill for the condominium has not been paid, the electricity has been cut off." We tested our intercom and the stairwell lights in the block and, sure enough, they had no power. We phoned the agency again, who promised to investigate.

The agency called us back later that day to explain that although our landlord had paid his condominium fees, "someone" had not paid the electricity bill. This would be paid immediately. Reassured, I asked how long it would take for the communal area power to come back on.

"Maybe three or four weeks." I sensed the agent shrug down the phone. "It will be whenever they have another reason to be in the area. They won't make a visit just to do a two minute job."

Brilliant. We spent the next four weeks with no doorbell or stairwell lighting. A great deal of stumbling around and groping our way up the stairs at night by the light of our mobile phones ensued. Hanging around on the front balcony at 1.30 pm for the post-lady to arrive became a habit, in case she had anything for us that was too large to fit in the letterbox. As the sun had begun to shine again and it was as warm outside as in the peak of English summer, neither of us grumbled about this too much.

Missing England

I missed England a lot less than I expected. Instead I was excited to be living in Portugal and being part of a different culture. However, there were one or two things that I did miss.

I missed understanding what people were saying to me. More than that, I missed knowing that it was me they were speaking to in the first place. Having my hair done was the worst for this – the hairdresser would speak while her eyes were focused on what she was doing to my hair. Without understanding what she had said, I couldn't be sure whether she was speaking to me, to the customers in the waiting area or to one of her fellow hairdressers. An awkward moment would follow, until thankfully the person she had spoken to answered.

I also missed certain things that I had taken for granted in England, such as being able to plug in an electrical item without fearing blue sparks would erupt from the socket.

There were certain foods that I missed, but our regular work trips back to England meant that I still got to gorge on sausage rolls, fish and chips and taramasalata, albeit with less frequency than before we emigrated.

The two things I missed most (aside from face to face contact with family and friends, of course) were carpets and central heating. After the coldness of our first winter in Portugal, being able to step out of bed onto a soft, fluffy carpet

65

had become something I remembered fondly. Somehow, stepping onto ice-cold floor tiles first thing in the morning just wasn't the same. Thankfully my ever-practical father sent me a pair of lovely, warm boot-slippers and the carpet issue was promptly forgotten.

The lack of central heating was not something that could be so easily overcome. I missed it for both its room-warming and clothes-drying functions, but in a rental property there was nothing I could do. Luckily as the weather finally began to warm up, I was able to cast off my English longing for radiators and focus instead on what I didn't miss about England.

London's rush-hour traffic was definitely top of the list of things I didn't miss. In England I had often spent hours getting to work and home again. In Portugal, I had to walk into my living room and open my laptop. Instead of arriving at work stressed out and annoyed, I started every day in fine form, ready for an effective and productive day at work.

I also didn't miss the type of people I used to encounter in London – money-obsessed city-types whose values would never be at one with my slightly more hippy, beach-loving attitude. I'm not saying their values were wrong and mine were right – they just weren't compatible and it was refreshing after so many years to move to a country where family life and happiness were put before money. My pace of life slowed down and I felt happier for it.

Other than the odd item of food, I also found I didn't really miss my English diet. Due to the hours we had worked in England, we would get home stupidly late and have takeaway or microwave meals at least twice each week. In Portugal, we ate fish caught early that morning and bought from the market for a couple of euros. We ate seasonal produce that had been grown locally, instead of shipped to the supermarket from the other side of the world. It was a very different way of eating than we were used to and we embraced it fully (although I must confess I did have the occasional secret craving for a Gregg's sausage roll). We also drank good wine that cost at most €4 per bottle – and that was for the really expensive stuff, so I didn't miss English wine prices at all.

I didn't miss the higher cost of living in England either – we had paid £200 a month Council Tax in London, while in Portugal we paid nothing. By moving abroad, we had saved enough in Council Tax alone to buy 50 bottles of wine each month. Not that we spent all of the money saved on wine, but it was an impressive argument in Portugal's favour!

One final thing that I definitely did not miss about England was our former neighbour's awful piano playing. When played well, the piano can be an instrument of great subtlety and beauty. Sadly nobody seemed to have told our neighbour that. She used to play loudly and badly at least twice each day and sometimes more. Although charmed by her persistence at first, after seven years of living next door to her it had seriously begun to grate on my nerves.

Overall, life in the Algarve was definitely better than it had been in London. We didn't miss anything too much and were happy to live with the occasional pang of homesickness for something from our former country, if it meant we got to live out our dream life by the beach. If we did find ourselves temporarily moping around over something no longer attainable, we would just jump in the car and go to discover something new instead – like driving up a mountain.

Woods and mountains

We had noticed several signposts to Mata de Conceição (Conceição Woods) near our new village and were curious to explore more of our local area. After some quick research on the web, which warned us about the presence of snakes, we set off wearing long trousers and sturdy shoes. The photographs on the Internet had not been particularly inspiring, but we had a couple of hours to spare so thought we would go and see for ourselves what the woods had to offer.

Despite the abundance of signposts, the woods were surprisingly hard to find. After taking the first turning, we wound our way along country lanes, through orange groves and pretty little villages in the hills, but then emerged back on the main road. Taking the next turning at which the woods were signposted led us in a second large, twisting circle back to the main road.

Our third attempt proved successful and we turned into the woods on a bumpy dirt track. Our hire car, a tiny hatchback, bounced along collecting mud, leaves and scratches from the bushes crowding the narrow track. (Added to the fact that I had dented the car the previous week, whilst reversing down a cobbled alleyway to make way for an impatient local, our accidental "off-roading" meant we were none to keen to return the car at the end of the hire period.)

We persevered, partly because the track was too narrow

to turn around in and partly because we had the comfort of knowing we had paid for extra insurance when hiring the car (phew!). After about five minutes, the track widened and we caught a glimpse of water between the trees. We stopped the car and went to investigate. A quick wander led us to the edge of a beautiful lake, hidden away in the centre of the woods and invisible to the outside world. It was a stunning site and not something we had expected to see in the Algarve – it looked so English in its setting amongst the trees.

After drinking in the beauty of the hidden lake, accompanied by the birdsong and the drone of nearby bees, we carried on through the woods. Stands of almond trees enchanted us, their white blossom, with the tiniest hint of pastel pink, drifting like snowflakes in the breeze. We were delighted to have found such unexpected beauty so close to home.

The scene called to mind an old Portuguese legend about the almond trees. It is said that long ago, before Portugal became a country, there was a famous Moorish warrior king. Amongst his prisoners he came across the beautiful Gilda – a princess captured from a foreign land. The king was smitten and, over the years, won Gilda's trust until she agreed to become his wife.

After many happy years, Gilda became sick and the king could find nothing to cure her. An elderly prisoner from Gilda's homeland begged an audience with the king and informed him that the cause of the sickness was that Gilda missed the snows of her home country. The king formed a plan and planted almond trees all over his country.

In spring, the king took his beloved Gilda out onto the castle's balcony. When she saw the almond flowers fluttering through the air, so much like her longed-for snow, Gilda at once began to recover from her illness. Her health recovered, Gilda and the king spent many happy years together, always waiting eagerly for the spring with its almond blossom snowfall.

*

Upon leaving the woods, it quickly became clear that we were lost. Instead of heading home we appeared to be driving up a mountain. Steep, winding roads, some without any side barriers, gave views across incredible valleys full of orange, lemon, olive and almond trees. Breath-taking vista gave way to breath-taking vista as we twisted and turned our way ever higher, stunned by the views and not caring in the slightest that we had no idea where we were.

Just before sunset, we emerged from the mountains near Altura, a beach resort near the Spanish border. Locals were gathered on the sands and at the beach's little restaurant, all squeezing the last few drops out of the day, just as we were. It was an idyllic sunset and once more we had to remind ourselves that this was where we actually lived. The weather had warmed up and the scent of spring was in the air, with the promise of all the excitement that our first summer in our new country would bring.

The combination of our new home and the increasing sunshine felt like a true fresh start. Although we had enjoyed many good times in our first four months, living in the "mould zone" (as Ben named it) had taken its toll. Waking up with sore throats from breathing in spores and bleach was not part of the dream, and now that that had been removed it felt as if our adventure could begin in earnest.

Culture shock

Shortly after moving to the apartment, we had to return to England for a week for work. We were amazed at how alien some aspects of being in London felt. There were so many people and they were all in such a hurry! In just four months we had turned from fast-paced Londoners into those bumbling people who get in everyone's way at the entrance to the tube station. It took quite a force of will to up our pace to that of our previous life.

The number of signs telling us to do things (or not do things) also astonished us – how had we never noticed before just how many of them there were? In Portugal, health and safety essentially relies on people having common sense. During our first week in our new village, we had wandered down to the seafront after dark. A new boardwalk was being built along the length of the seafront and diggers, piles of rubble and building tools just sat about waiting for the crew to start work again the next morning. Nothing was fenced off. There were no warning signs anywhere. Even the large open manhole in our path, which Ben steered me away from at the last second, did not have barriers up. The Portuguese attitude to all this was simple – if you don't have enough common sense to not fall down an open manhole, it's your own silly fault (even if it is dark and the street is badly lit). In England, the whole area would have been boarded off, with numerous

71

signs warning about the dangers and the need to wear hard hats and protective goggles.

Little differences also caught our attention, particularly in shops and restaurants. English people at the tills in the supermarket queue up neatly, using the little placard supplied by the supermarket to separate their goods on the conveyor belt from the next person's. Portuguese people crowd around and pile their goods onto the belt, ignoring the little placard and instead preferring to challenge the checkout assistant to work out whose shopping is whose.

We also found ourselves having to think for a split second before saying words like please, thank you and hello. It seemed that certain Portuguese words were becoming fully ingrained in our brains at last! Portuguese habits had also become part of our life. As we walked down the street, we smiled at strangers and said good morning to elderly passers by. The scowls and funny looks we received in return reminded us quickly that this was not the done thing in London!

Overall, London had become a bit of a culture shock – far more so than we would have expected after just a few months. The pace of life and the noise and dirt of being in such a big city made us even more grateful for our little Portuguese village, with its swallows singing as they darted through the evening air catching insects and its frogs croaking out their mating calls along the river.

Playing house

Glad to be back in Portugal, we spent some time "playing house", now that we could relax in our new apartment. Lazy, wine-soaked evenings on the balcony were essential, now that the weather had begun to improve, so we set about furnishing it with plants and other garden bits and pieces. Although my preference is for growing fruit and vegetables, the Portuguese love growing flowers, so my tomato plants and lettuces were interspersed with colourful blossoms and sweet-scented jasmine.

While I was thrilled to spend hours traipsing round garden centres, for Ben it was all about the barbecue and the pursuit of his much-yearned-for Weber. When we lived in England, the weather and our interfering neighbours didn't permit us to barbecue much (one neighbour would slam all her windows shut to keep the smoke out before we had even lit the charcoal). Now that we lived in the sun, it was Weber time. Thus one Sunday morning we set off to tour the garden and home stores in Faro. Our quest was not as simple as we had hoped. The first two shops we visited didn't stock any Webers and we were feeling a little dejected when we entered the third one, but there it was – the king of barbecues! Gas powered and with cute folding side tables, places to hang cooking implements and a funky stand, it called out to Ben, who was powerless to resist. Half an hour later, Weber safely in the boot of the car, we headed back home to try it out, planning to grab a gas bottle at the nearest petrol station on the way.

Unfortunately it turned out that buying a gas bottle was much harder than buying the actual barbeque. It being Sunday, some of the petrol stations were closed. In those that were open, staff fired off rapid Portuguese at us, telling us that we needed a different brand of gas than they stocked, or a different colour gas bottle. Poor Ben's blood pressure rose a little more with each encounter.

We finally found a petrol station with the right brand and right colour bottles. Marching expectantly up to the counter, we explained our needs. With much arm waving and head shaking, the assistant conveyed the message that the green gas bottles outside were empty – she didn't have any full ones at the moment. And so we drove to our fifth petrol station of the day – the last one in the local area. Thankfully they had the bottle we needed and Ben's blood pressure slowly began to fall again as we drove home with everything we needed.

Once the glorious Weber had been installed, we popped to the supermarket for some provisions (anything that could be barbecued; not a salad leaf in sight) and Ben cooked up a feast on our new, plant- and sunshine-filled balcony. It was to be the first of many such happy events.

*

The same week that we purchased the barbecue, our broadband was finally installed. After four months of stupid paperwork-related irritation, we finally had decent Internet, cable TV and a home phone line. I also had big plans to watch Portuguese children's TV to help with my language-learning efforts. I was hoping for a Portuguese equivalent of Sesame Street, but most of the children's programmes seemed aimed at a slightly older audience (of at least six). Having stared blankly at the screen for 20 minutes and not understood a single word, I reluctantly accepted that I could understand less than the average six-year-old.

Friends frequently asked us how our Portuguese was coming along (after they had asked the obligatory question about the weather). Despite being unable to understand cartoons, we were actually not doing too badly with the basics. Ordering train tickets, going to restaurants and asking for directions had become second nature. We also had to use the Internet much less when it came to things like reading recipes or deciphering cooking instructions on packets of food. Some things, like using the cashpoint to get money out and pay our household bills, were managed by our brains without any hint of translation at all – as we had learned how to do it in Portuguese first.

One thing that helped massively with our language learning was the friendliness of the Portuguese people. Our simple attempts at communication were very much appreciated and people were always happy to help us learn if we didn't know the word for something. The surprised smiles when we spoke in Portuguese were a sad reminder that many of our fellow Brits living in Portugal did not even bother to learn the basics.

Verbs and grammar still proved tricky, as did the distinctive Algarve dialect, although we did better at picking up the latter after we started imitating our neighbours and the staff in our local shop. Speaking Portuguese, particularly in the Algarve, often involves chopping off the beginning and end of words when you say them – and sometimes missing them out of the sentence altogether if they are little words. Thus, the three syllables of *tudo bem?* which we had carefully learned from our language CDs (an informal greeting meaning "all well?"), became "dooong-bayng" with two syllables at most.

The difference between written Portuguese and spoken Portuguese is quite astonishing, but we were slowly beginning to spot patterns in words and phrases and have some idea of how to pronounce words that we saw written down.

Our improving language skills led to another problem – the more convincingly we spoke Portuguese, the more likely the person we were talking to was to fire something back at us as if we spoke the language fluently. Conversations became a focused exercise, with both of us desperately trying to pick out the one or two words that we recognised and then make up the rest of the speaker's sentence to fit these words. Understandably, this process was a little hit and miss. Ben was much better at working out what people had said, while I was a bit more advanced at speaking – so we could just about manage a conversation with someone if we pooled our skills and focused very hard.

Still, there was no doubt that we were making progress, and friends who came to stay with us from England for the second time remarked on how much better our language skills were since their last visit, which was really pleasing.

*

Late March brought with it the wonderful scent of orange blossom. Going to our local beach meant a ten minute walk past groves of trees in bloom, the air filled with their sweet, heady scent. It was not something that we had ever experienced before and it smelled heavenly. We wandered past the groves as often as possible.

Sadly, the smell of the orange trees was not the only thing to fill the air – mosquitoes also appeared in droves as April approached. While Ben received a few token bites, it was me they really wanted. Friends and relatives suggested various ways to avoid them (take vitamin B6 tablets, eat bananas, eat Marmite daily, don't eat any Marmite ever), all of which I tried. However, the mosquitoes were not to be deterred.

I don't really help myself with bites, in that I do tend to scratch them, but as I've never had an allergic reaction, it's never been a problem. On previous holidays to Portugal I had been bitten many times. So when my bites started swelling it didn't immediately occur to me that I was having a reaction. I carried on scratching them (when Ben wasn't looking, so as to avoid being told off). There was one near my elbow that was particularly itchy and I scratched it obsessively. It swelled more and the itching suddenly began spreading up my entire arm. My elbow bone disappeared into a tight mound of puffy flesh and I couldn't bend my arm fully. The skin all the way from my wrist to my shoulder burned. After a few days, the pain and the crawling sensation under my skin got so bad that I couldn't sleep at night.

The only positive part of all this was that I got to practise the "going to the chemist" module of my Portuguese language CD. Chemists' in Portugal are fantastic places. You can buy a vast range of drugs over the counter without a prescription and the majority of them are cheaper than paying a standard NHS prescription charge in the UK. There are exceptions, of course – Lemsip or anything like it is not sold here and cough medicine can cost up to €15 per bottle. For anything other than the common cold though, Portuguese chemists are wonderful.

Two packets of antihistamine tablets and one tube of antihistamine cream later, my giant arm returned to normal and I was finally able to get a good night's sleep.

The Ecovia

With the sun shining almost every day now, we were full of energy and ready to introduce exercise into our lives – something we had talked about but consistently failed to do during our last decade in London.

Our local supermarket had an offer on for bicycles at €50 each. I've never been a keen cyclist (my sense of balance leaves something to be desired) but the pretty purple ladies' bike, which had room for a basket on the front, was too good to resist. I had visions of cycling around the village in the early morning, basket filled with fresh bread and olives. (Ben found it very funny that I was far more excited about having a basket to put things in than about having the actual bicycle.)

Ben was keen to discover the Ecovia – a cycle route which stretches the full length of the Algarve, from Sagres in the west to Vila Real de Santo António on the Spanish border in the east. The route is marked with little painted arrows and runs primarily along dedicated cycle paths or traffic-calmed back roads. In true Portuguese style it is not always quite clear where the route goes next and some element of guesswork has to be employed, but for us that was all part of the fun. On our first weekend with the new bikes we tried two stretches of it.

Our first route was quite short. We cycled through fields and meadows, then into the Ria Formosa nature reserve and in between the salt pans. The route was mainly flat, which was perfect for our first ride (I've never been very good at cycling up hills). It was a gorgeous time of year – the heavy winter rains (now thankfully a distant memory) meant that the springtime meadows had exploded with little yellow flowers, which stretched as far as the eye could see.

Upon reaching Tavira, we had a couple of drinks in the afternoon sun, before heading back as darkness was approaching. This turned out to be a bad idea. As dusk descended, so did clouds of mosquitoes, whizzing around the marshy ground either side of the cycle path and feasting on my blood. Being a rather wobbly cyclist, slapping them away was out of the question – instead we cycled as hard as we could, then celebrated reaching home by cracking open yet another packet of antihistamine tablets.

Our bike ride the following day, to the beach of Manta Rota and back, was a longer and more challenging route. As two unfit people with a fondness for food and wine, we struggled a little with the hot sun beating down on us as we cycled around our village trying to find the next set of direction arrows. After a wiggling detour through the village and over the railway line, we found the arrows and set off along the dirt tracks and minor roads, winding through fields of olive and almond trees and fragrant orange groves. The whole ride was a wonderful assault on the senses, with the heady scent of orange blossom combining with the faintly aniseed-like smell of wild fennel. We sailed downhill past luxurious golf courses, maintained to perfection and stunning to look at. Sadly, having gone down one hill, we had to head back up the next one. A series of challenging hills followed until we had passed the tiny fishing village of Fabrica and the beautiful little hamlet of Cacela Velha. The hills between Cacela and Manta Rota were even steeper than those we had already passed and we dearly regretted all those evenings of "just one more glass of wine".

It was worth the pain when we arrived in Manta Rota and

could refresh our hot, tired feet in the sea, before settling down to a long lunch of razor clam rice and local green wine in a café.

The journey back was even harder work, because of our full stomachs, and involved quite a few rest stops. Despite our tiredness and achy limbs, as we cycled back onto our road with the sun setting to our left, we felt sad to be putting our bikes away – like young children who have to go home to bed at the end of a summer's day.

We determined that we would cycle more of the beautiful Ecovia (Ben had already begun to work out how long it would take to cover the whole distance, with overnight stops along the way), but not until our sore bits had recovered! However, the time of long, relaxing weekend bike rides came to a swift end – the visitor season was about to begin!

Visitors

April was a busy month. We had three sets of visitors back-to-back, with just enough time in between to race around cleaning the apartment and putting fresh linen on the beds.

Having so many of our nearest and dearest visit in such a short space of time was both exhausting and wonderful and we thoroughly enjoyed catching up on all the gossip about life back in England. Sharing the sites and culture of our new life made us appreciate it afresh. We introduced people to their first taste of Iberico ham, shared a range of potent Portuguese liqueurs (sadly so potent that I spent a good two hours wrapped around the toilet one evening) and joined some of our closest friends on their first expedition to the beach with their eight-month-old-baby. Perhaps predictably enough, baby Jacob's first instinct was to see what sand tasted like – but he quickly learned that it was more fun to play with than to eat. Watching him taste his first olive was truly magical as well!

After building our routine around just the two of us living in our apartment, having guests to stay always took a little getting used to, but was also a welcome change. When they left, the apartment would feel strangely empty and quiet, and it would take a couple of days to readjust to being on our own again.

One thing we quickly learned is that when people come to visit, they are very much on holiday. They intend to eat, drink and spend at holiday pace the whole time they are here.

Despite both enjoying our jobs immensely, suddenly the days on which we had to work would feel like torture, as we were missing out on the infectious holiday fun going on all around us. Our livers and waistlines suffered and strict regimes of salad-eating and alcohol-free days had to take over as soon as guests left. Our wallets also suffered, as night after night in restaurants and bars took their toll. By the time our third set of guests arrived in April, we had already spent all the month's money and shuddered at the thought of having to eat out again so soon.

Despite our lack of funds and over-indulgence, it was a great month. We bobbed around in the (surprisingly warm) Atlantic in giant rubber rings for hours on end. We watched fish swimming in the wave tops. We learnt how to prepare and cook fresh squid from the local fish market. We sat outside drinking wine on warm, balmy evenings and enjoying the company of old friends.

Finally, the last of our guests went home and, after a whistle-stop tour to England for a wedding and a few days' work, we were able to rest our stomachs, livers and wallets for a few weeks before our next guests were due to arrive.

Becoming Portuguese

By the time we had lived in Portugal for six months, we were referring to it as "home". Our life in the sun had become normal. Shopping at the market and supermarket, which had at first seemed so strange as a result of all the different products and cuts of meat, was just part of the routine. Seeing whole skinned rabbits on the meat counter and chickens with their feet or heads still on no longer felt unusual (although we had yet to attempt cooking a whole rabbit).

Our recent trip back to England had made me realise how truly we had settled in Portugal, as I found myself feeling homesick for the Algarve. We had no regrets about our new life and our steady flow of visitors, coupled with catching up with everyone when we went back to England for work, meant that our worries about missing friends and family were entirely unfounded.

We did miss little things (foods mainly), but the bright sunshine pouring into the apartment every morning when I opened the shutters more than made up for the things we had to do without.

Our language skills had improved. When we first made the move, our attempts at interaction in Portuguese were nervous and often met with baffled stares. It had not helped that Ben's default, panicked reaction when he could not find the right Portuguese phrase was to start speaking French! With practice, though, we had become capable of managing every-day conversations and were no longer floundering quite so much, even if we did still have a long way to go.

The friendly and welcoming spirit of the Portuguese people was much more suited to our personalities than the often tense atmosphere of London. Their support of my attempts to learn their language (if sometimes coupled with gentle amusement) was so encouraging and each day brought some small triumph.

The cost of life in Portugal was something we had begun to take for granted. Travelling, eating and drinking in London seemed ridiculously overpriced. After paying £100 for our share of a (relatively mediocre) meal out with friends in central London, not counting the drinks before and after or the £35 taxi back to our hotel, we appreciated afresh the Portuguese restaurants providing as much fish as you could eat for €9 per head.

Our changed lifestyle, with commuting removed, meant we had a great deal more time than we used to. We read more, baked more and Ben became a keen spring-onion grower. Happily, we also spent a great deal more time at the beach.

We had become more Portuguese in several little ways, unnoticed to us until visitors from England pointed them out. We ate dinner much later, sometimes not starting cooking until after 10 pm. We preferred going to the market early on a Saturday morning and having coffee with the locals rather than going out drinking on a Friday night. We knew that a knock on the door at 11 pm was not a cause for alarm, but more likely to be a visit from a neighbour – often bearing a cake or a bowl of freshly picked figs.

Ben analysed the changes on his blog, looking at how we thought we might feel before the move, versus how we actually felt after having lived in Portugal for six months. Before we moved, we had worried about missing friends and family, whether the locals would welcome and accept us, whether we would miss the changing seasons of English weather, get bored of fresh fish or miss London. Our main worry had been that life in Portugal would not live up to our romantic notions.

After six months, we were able to look back on all of our fears and preconceptions, happy in the knowledge that they had been mostly unfounded. The combination of technology and frequent visits meant that we maintained contact with our friends and family. We did not miss English weather in the slightest, and had very quickly begun to take the sunshine for granted. We had been welcomed into our new country and supported by the locals in our attempts to integrate. We hadn't really managed to implement a fitness regime, but we did eat more healthily, taking advantage of local, seasonal produce. We did *not* miss London.

So, despite taking some things for granted, we both still felt very lucky to have had the opportunity to move here. Naturally there was a downside too – but as it consisted mainly of being constantly bitten by mosquitoes and paying more for electricity, I was more than happy to make the trade. We had exchanged money for happiness and a simpler life. It had not been a mistake.

Having said which, we were about to hit some bumps in the road.

Red tape

By May, we knew we had to once more face the ordeal of Portuguese paperwork. It was time to get our *residência* sorted out. As European citizens we had the right to live and work anywhere in the EU, but needed to formalise the arrangement by getting our documents in order. Our farcical experience of obtaining fiscal numbers meant that we had delayed this for as long as we could, but it was finally time to tackle it. A lot of English people living in Portugal adopt a policy of "staying under the radar", meaning they don't apply for *residência* (which legally they have to) and in some cases don't even obtain fiscal numbers. Given that we had moved here intending to stay permanently, and being the kind of people who like to do things properly, this was not an option for us.

Ben did a lot of research online – days' and days' worth. He read the Portuguese government's website, the *Finanças* website, the SEF (Serviço de Estrangeiros e Fronteiras – the Portuguese equivalent of the UK Border Agency) website, the EU website and numerous expat forums. The results were not promising. Although EU law was clear, it seemed that each *câmara* (town hall) in Portugal had interpreted it in its own quirky way and that even different officials within the same *câmara* would provide different instructions. Our lives became consumed with gathering together the right paperwork in order to satisfy all of our local *câmara's* requirements.

The fact that we both had incomes from the UK did not help, as this meant we could not obtain Portuguese social security numbers. To obtain a social security number in Portugal, you either have to be employed by a Portuguese company or be self employed. We were neither. I was employed by an English company and Ben owned his own English company. The Portuguese system simply had no place for us.

After much painstaking effort, we finally had a clear plan and had put together a folder full of what seemed to be the required documents. It was time to obtain our *residência*.

First we went to the *Finanças* to change the address on our fiscal numbers from our Tavira property to our new one. It took five minutes, which we (naively) took as an omen that this round of paperwork was going to go smoothly.

Next we drove to the *Loja do Cidadão* (citizens' shop) in Tavira. We took a number from the ticket machine and waited. When our number was called, the lady behind the counter told us that we would have to go to either the *câmara* or the SEF office. We tried SEF first, only to find out they were closed for the day as it was past 3.00 pm. Next we tried the *câmara*.

Initially things seemed to be going well. Although nobody spoke any English, I had been practising the phrases I would need and the woman behind the counter seemed to understand what we wanted. She pulled out two forms and circled items on a list of documents that we would need to produce. We hastily pulled out the folder and provided her with passports, fiscal numbers, recent photographs and my contract of employment. She examined all of them (frowning deeply when I explained that my contract of employment was with an English company and thus written in English), before circling another item on the list: *atestado*. A quick consultation with my pocket dictionary explained that this meant "certificate". Hmm.

Through a combination of gestures and repetition, the lady behind the counter managed to explain to us that we needed to go to the *junta de freguesia* (a kind of mini village hall/post office) in our local village in order to obtain a certificate to say where we lived. Finally understanding, I triumphantly produced our tenancy agreement for the apartment, along with a bill with our name and address on it. If the *câmara* needed proof of address then surely that would be fine?

The woman shook her head.

"*Atestado,*" she said again.

By this stage our choice Portuguese phrases had been exhausted and we were left trying to stutteringly argue that surely a tenancy agreement was proof of address.

"*Atestado.*" She shrugged.

Accepting defeat (temporarily) we stuffed our documents back in the folder, along with the two forms she had given us, and headed back to our village.

The village hall was, surprisingly, open (most government offices seem to close for lunch for a couple of hours and then close for the day at around 3.30 pm). We marched in, folder in hand, and explained what we needed. The lady behind the counter took our passports and fiscal numbers, then looked over our tenancy agreement. She handed us a form.

We filled out our details, but got stuck at the signature boxes as there were two and we weren't sure which one to sign. I asked, but the woman shook her head and explained that we had to ask two residents of the village, who had to be Portuguese and registered voters, to sign the form to prove we lived in the village. Having not lived there for very long, we explained that we didn't know anyone here and asked if two of our many acquaintances in Tavira could sign the form. Another shake of the head.

Sensing Ben about to explode beside me (paperwork and awkward officials are a combination he hates with a passion),

I thanked the lady, grabbed all of our documents, including the two additional forms, and headed out the door. We drove home in silence, Ben's fury filling the void left by the absence of conversation. We didn't speak until we had each got a beer and gone out to sit in the sun on our front balcony. It was Ben who finally broke the silence:

"I think I'm going to look at the price of flats in Brighton."

Making friends

The village hall's requirement that two local voters sign our *atestado* application form got me thinking about making friends. It wasn't something I had ever had to give much thought to before. As a child at school, you just make friends. Everyone tends to be new at the same time and it isn't an issue. At university it was the same. Once in the workplace, the daily routine and after-work drinks further expand your circle of friends. You also get to know people through friends of friends.

When we moved to Portugal we knew nobody. We weren't bothered as we enjoy our own company and were excited about our adventure. However, the *atestado* debacle made us realise that, after six months here, we hadn't really made any proper friends. We had a great many acquaintances – people we knew from the local bar and would go out for meals with or have over to ours for barbecues – but not the type of friends we had back home.

One problem was the age gap. Portuguese people of our age (early thirties) were generally married and at home taking care of their children. We did not have children, so meeting and befriending people our own age was not easily achieved. The culture was another issue. In Portugal it is common for people to socialise with their extended family. Although they are very welcoming to outsiders, opportunities to integrate do not often arise.

The fact that we both worked from home further reduced our opportunity to meet people. If we worked in offices we would meet make new acquaintances amongst those we worked with, but this did not apply. The only person from our village that we met while working from home was the post lady.

Our only having moved to the village a couple of months ago was a further obstacle, as did the fact that it's a really small place – there weren't exactly a great many people to choose from. We could have easily found two Portuguese voters who would sign our form in Tavira, but it seemed we would have to set about making friends in our new village.

Ben's fury at how difficult the Portuguese were making it for us to obtain the documents we were entitled to as EU citizens led to me taking matters into my own hands. My first idea was to call one of the numerous document agencies that had been recommended by people on the expat forums. I spoke to a nice lady, who demanded even more documents than the *câmara*, including a certified copy of our wedding certificate translated into Portuguese. Having got married in Antigua, I knew that this would not be straightforward, so the document agency idea was abandoned immediately.

For Plan B, I used Google Translate to write out a detailed explanation of what I needed and, armed with this, cycled to the little row of village shops.

I tried the launderette first but, after listening to me read out my carefully prepared speech, the ladies there shrugged and said they did not live locally.

The local shop was next on my list. The shop was a thriving hub of village life, where locals gathered to exchange the latest news and gossip and occasionally buy something. That day was no exception. The shopkeeper interrupted her conversation with three local ladies and asked if she could help me. I read out my speech. The shopkeeper looked confused, so I handed her the piece of paper. She read it and then began an animated conversation with her customers, none of which I understood. Hopefully, I held out my *atestado* form.

The lovely shopkeeper signed the form and copied her voter number onto it from a kind of voting registration card that she kept in her wallet. I held the form out to the ladies gathered in the shop and smiled in supplication, but they declined to take it, looking at me with suspicion. The shop lady waved her voter card, pointed at the ladies and shook her head. I understood – nobody else had their voter card with them, so could not sign the form. I was elated nonetheless – my mission was 50% complete.

My next stop was the bar opposite the shop. There were two bars in the village at the time – a forbidding one filled with scary looking old men who stared at passing pedestrians all day, and a rather less dingy one that attracted less intimidating locals, a few tourists and seemingly the whole village whenever football was on. Heading to the better-lit of the two establishments, I ordered a beer and read my speech to the manager. He said he would be happy to sign my form, but needed to get his voter card from home. I bought him a beer and promised to return later that day when he had had a chance to pop home. Four hours later, I went back and he signed the form, complete with voter number.

I returned home that evening triumphantly waving the signed *atestado* form. Ben was still annoyed, having reconfirmed on the Internet in the meantime that EU law gave us the right to live and work in Portugal anyway, but at least he stopped looking at flats for rent in Brighton.

Success (sort of)

On Monday I headed back to the village hall, signed forms in hand. The woman there took them, stamped them and told me to come back in a week. One week later, we received our official *atestado* documents. We now had the proof we needed to apply for our *residência*, so trekked back to the *câmara* in Tavria, our ever-growing folder of documents in hand.

Passports, fiscal numbers, photographs, contract of employment and *atestado* certificates were duly handed over, along with our completed and signed *residência* application forms. The woman behind the counter then asked for our social security numbers. We explained that we didn't have them. She explained that we needed them. We explained again that we didn't have them and the conversation began to go round in circles. Ben's blood pressure began to rise.

Finally, whether because she could see that Ben was about to blow, or for some other unknown reason, the woman took all our documents off to be photocopied. Our forms were stamped and initialled and we were provided with a copy. She told us to come back in a week and collect our *residência* documents. We returned home, wary of celebrating until we had the actual documents in hand.

A week later, I returned to the *câmara* and collected and paid for our *residência* certificates. It was a joyous occasion, but sadly the elation only lasted about ten minutes. We went straight from the *câmara* to the bank to register our change of address (the bank still had our English address on record from when we had opened the accounts). After spending ten minutes tapping details into the computer, the bank lady noticed that the address on our *residência* certificates did not match the address on our *atestado* or fiscal number documents – the *câmara* had mistyped our address.

Leaving Ben in a café with a beer, for fear he would do physical damage to the officials in the *câmara* if he had to return there, I went back and explained the situation. The woman examined the documents, shrugged, took our *residência* certificates away and told me to come back in a week. Defeated, I collected Ben and returned home.

One week later – and over a month since the whole process had begun – I returned to Tavira *câmara* to collect our *residência* certificates, which were now showing the correct address. I noticed that instead of the five year certificates we were supposed to receive, they had been dated to expire in a year.

Unable to face any more dealings with the *câmara* I thanked the woman and bolted from the building, safe in the knowledge that I wouldn't have to go back there for nearly a whole year. It had been a soul-destroying process and had consumed our lives throughout, but we had finally obtained the documents that it was our legal right to have all along. Although still determined to do things by the book, I did now have a much greater understanding of those expats who decided to simply slip under the radar. Still, we had risen to the challenge of facing Portuguese bureaucracy and had won the battle (if not the war). Now we could relax and enjoy the summer.

Party time

July and August saw summer truly arrive in the Algarve, with temperatures frequently topping 40°C in the day and remaining above 25°C at night. It was hot. With the heat came the tourists – well-heeled Portuguese tourists from Lisbon, large, noisy groups from Spain and the inevitable planeloads of Brits.

The Algarve responded by turning into a party zone. Not just at weekends, but every night of the week. Travelling markets roamed from one end of the Algarve to the other, often not opening their stalls until midnight when the ferocious heat backed off for a few hours. A huge clubbing tent was erected at Manta Rota beach. An abandoned water park became a nightclub for two months. The circus came to town.

The quiet, tranquil village we had moved into had transformed. By day, tourists raced to be the first to claim the sun loungers around our pool. By night, huge groups of people flocked to the seafront to drink and dance in the bars and to join the all-night beach parties.

So what did we do? We joined in, of course. We drank. We danced on tables. We jumped in the pool at 3.00 am to cool down after the ten-minute walk home. Then we drank some more. For five or six weeks of our first Portuguese summer, this became our life (well, at weekends anyway – we still had to work during the week).

Eventually the novelty of our village's transformation wore off. We grew tired of being too hung-over to go to the beach on Saturday. We got sick of the same tacky tourist songs playing over and over in the village bars. We realised that the dancing on the table in the bar was not a spontaneous, "isn't this a brilliant night" moment, but something encouraged by the bar staff to make people think that. We remembered that we were no longer in our twenties and that, unlike most of the party people surrounding us, we were not here on holiday.

Abandoning the party lifestyle meant we had the energy and cash to enjoy Portugal in other ways, like diving through the waves in the sea and eating clams dripping with buttery sauce as the sun set over the beach. The apartment smelled constantly of sun cream and even our dry skin, stingy from too many dips in the sea, was a pleasure.

We were grateful that we had chosen to live at the eastern end of the Algarve. However lively our own end was, it was nothing compared to the more westerly resorts such as Albufeira, which had become a true hellhole. After an ill-advised trip to Praia da Rocha in late July, we retreated eastwards and resolved firmly to remain there until at least mid-September.

The hot weather often made sleeping difficult over the summer months. We would fall asleep with the air con running full blast, then wake up shivering two hours later and turn it off. Half an hour later we would wake up sweating and turn it back on. Being dive-bombed by whining mosquitoes also didn't help. Maybe this was why the Portuguese seemed to opt for staying up all night throughout the summer.

As well as the planeloads of tourists, the summer sun also attracted some more friends and family members to stay with us. My Dad kindly treated us to a trip to Zoomarine – a sea-life-based theme park with an aquarium, swimming pool, fairground rides and various animal shows and displays. The dolphin show was particularly amazing – the dolphins and trainers seemed utterly in tune with each other, sharing a lot of love, and the dolphins seemed to love performing.

We found that Zoomarine placed a great deal of emphasis on caring for animals; the environment and the day were educational as well as great fun. The only bit I didn't like was the big wheel. I'm afraid of heights and looking back I can't really remember why I thought going on a big wheel would be a good idea. Ben and my Dad were keen though, so on we got. My brother and his girlfriend had conveniently disappeared at this point.

It was as we approached the full height of the wheel, with Ben pointing out the amazing views and me holding on for dear life with my eyes shut, that I realised that Dad was unusually quiet. I risked a quick peep at him and saw that, like me, he was clinging on with white knuckles to the centre pole in our carriage. He didn't say anything, but I suspect I now know who I got my fear of heights from. After three horrendous rotations, we were finally released and I fled from the carriage, much to the amusement of the line of people waiting to get on (and Ben).

It was good to do something new and different so close to home and despite our different ages and interests, all five of us had a great day. It reminded me that the Algarve still had so much we hadn't explored – let alone the rest of Portugal!

The rest of my family's holiday passed all too quickly. Ben and I had taken a few days off work and we all enjoyed stopping at numerous cafés and restaurants, as well as visiting some of our local beaches – although my Dad's not putting sun cream on his feet in the 40°C heat had very painful consequences.

My brother Rob and his girlfriend hired a pedalo with us at one of the beaches. These come with built-in slides, which looked like such fun we couldn't resist. It turned out to be a whole lot less straightforward than we had expected. Waves that had looked small and calm from the beach suddenly seemed huge, rocking the pedalo up and down and from side to side. Not what you need when trying to climb steps and then get onto a slide. Somehow we managed to return to shore with only minor injuries – a few bumps and bruises and a big lump on my foot where I managed to get it stuck under the pedalo's pedal.

We also tried out the electric mopeds being hired out on the seafront. The mopeds had pedals like a bicycle, but with an electric motor. As they were classified as bicycles, we were allowed to ride them on the Ecovia, meaning we could race along without having to worry about traffic. They were splendid fun, the only mishap being when I climbed off and tried to walk my bike round in a circle, accidentally turning the throttle whilst doing so and ending up on the floor in a heap, much to the amusement of my companions.

The highlight of the week was taking the family to the beautiful waterfall of Pego do Inferno, about 15 minutes from our apartment. The waterfall is slightly off the beaten track and a good way to escape the tourists. The crystal-clear water drops several metres into a deep pool, where we cooled our feet and swam, delighting in the fish swimming past our toes. A rope swing hung from a tree at the side of the waterfall and could be reached by clambering up some of the wet and slippery rocks. Youngsters were using it to swing out over the pool and then splash into the water below. My brother's girlfriend wanted to try it so I said I would go with her.

It hadn't looked that high from the ground, but by the time I had climbed up, my knees were shaking in fear – a sensation which I had heard of before but never experienced until that moment. The tiny rock platform, with jagged rocks below, suddenly seemed about a mile high. A local boy of about 15 was standing on the platform, kindly using a long bamboo stick to hook the rope swing back for each new jumper – a tricky feat given that it took both hands, meaning he couldn't hold on to the rocks while doing it.

Kat went first so there was no way I could back out without seeming a complete coward. The queue of people behind me also meant there was no way down other than to jump. I edged towards the tiny rock ledge. At that point I realised that the "kind" Portuguese boy was not just helping the jumpers out of altruism – in order to stand fully on the jumping rock, I had to straddle the grinning young man. I was suddenly very conscious that I was wearing nothing other than a skimpy bikini.

Finally I was past him. I gripped the bit of wood tied to the rope tightly in both hands and swung out over the water. I had planned a graceful drop (perhaps even a little somersault), but the moment my arms realised how heavy my body was gravity took over and I plummeted into the cold water below. Hardly the graceful dive I had envisioned.

I was thrilled to have actually done the jump and the sudden rush of adrenaline was most welcome, but it took a good ten minutes before my legs stopped feeling wobbly. Still, at least while queuing and waiting for our turn to jump Kat (who is Portuguese) taught me how to say, "I am afraid" in Portuguese – a phrase which the circumstances meant I was unlikely ever to forget.

Sadly when the family's visit came to an end we were once more left with an empty-feeling apartment and a backlog of work to get on with.

Excitingly though, my mother and some of my step-family, who had been pondering a move to Portugal for some time, seemed to have found a suitable property just half an hour's drive from our village. It appeared that we might have some family living nearby in the not-too-distant future.

The great outdoors

The beaches became very crowded over the summer, particularly during August, but we still swam in the sea at least twice a week. We delighted in the ever changing conditions that we encountered – the colour of the sky and the size and pattern of the waves was constantly shifting, meaning that the beach was a new experience every time.

On still days, when the water was crystal clear and tinged with shades of green, fish would dart around our legs as we paddled in the shallows or bobbed happily around for hours on one of our inflatables.

On other days, long, rolling waves would make the conditions perfect for body boarding – something which we had never tried before moving to Portugal, but which became an essential part of our lives during our first summer here.

Ben's favourite days were the ones when the waves were taller than us and would knock you off your feet if you tackled them wrong. On those days we would spend hours diving through them, falling backwards into them or just trying to remain on our feet. Sadly a misjudgment of one such wave led me to lose my bikini and prescription sunglasses all in one go. The bikini was swiftly recovered, so my dignity was preserved, but sadly my shades were gone for ever.

Sometimes we would take a Frisbee to the beach, sometimes the body board, sometimes a picnic. No day there was ever the same. We read books, went for long walks along the sand and drank cocktails sitting on mini chairs sunken into the sand outside a beach bar. Then, when we were hot from doing all of that, we would jump straight back into the waves.

We never got bored of our new beach life, but we did start to get bored of the tourists. Although it had been fun at first, the traffic jams, queuing for things and general noise everywhere had begun to grate on our nerves, even up our "quieter" end of the Algarve. Service in our favourite restaurants had become shambolic, we queued in traffic on roads that were usually barely used and shopping in the supermarket was like Christmas Eve every day.

By mid-August we were ready for them to disperse and give us back our roads, beaches and shops. We didn't want to wish our lives away, but we were very much looking forward to the start of September when some form of reality would return.

The Algarve's population is said to increase four-fold during the summer months, so perhaps it's not surprising that the infrastructure suffers somewhat. A huge proportion of the area's income is derived from tourism, and businesses have to make enough between June and August to keep them going for the rest of the year. All this said, it was still lovely when, during the first week in September, the tourists vanished en masse and we once more stood a chance of using our pool.

To combat the hordes during the height of the summer, we did our best to find local places that the tourists were unlikely to discover. One of these was the Ria Formosa nature reserve that ran between our village and Tavira. This beautiful and ever-changing landscape provided a haven of peace and tranquillity during the heady months of summer.

One weekend, we rambled across it on our way to Tavira, more for the walk and the peace and quiet than because we wanted anything from town. After a quick drink in Tavira we returned on the same route. The salt pans sparkled in the sun.

Over the past few months they had morphed from giant pools of water into hard beds of crystalline, glittering beauty.

We stopped to admire them on the way back, both of us a little ashamed that we still hadn't found out how salt was actually made and harvested, despite the salt pans causing us to debate this every time we walked past them.

The surface of the salt looked like a thick, sparkly crust. There were cracks in it, as though it had baked and dried out completely in the summer sun. Ben, being inquisitive at heart, wanted to touch the salt. He looked around for a stick with which to prod it, but there was nothing suitable to hand, so he starting edging gingerly down the muddy bank to poke it with his toe. Not sharing the boyish desire to prod the salt, I waited at the top.

Ben reached the salt and triumphantly reached one foot out, meaning to test its firmness. Within half a second he had slipped, sliding on his bottom from the bank into the salt. He discovered that under their cracked, seemingly parched surfaces, both the salt and the bank were actually extremely wet and muddy. His face was a mixture of surprise and panic, which quickly turned to dismay as he pulled himself up and caught sight of the huge brown mud-smear all the way down the back of his white shorts.

We were 20 minutes from home and although the nature reserve was deserted, the streets between the end of it and our apartment would certainly not be. Ben would have to walk back looking like he'd had a potty-training accident in his bright, white shorts.

Now, it might be mean of me, but the sight of people falling over unexpectedly tickles my funny bone. As soon as I established that Ben wasn't hurt, the giggles started to build up inside me. As he realised the extent of the muddy mess, Ben's dismay turned into irritation. I tried to help by wiping at the mud with a couple of spare carrier bags I had with me.

It didn't work – the stain spread, Ben got crosser and I had to bite my lip to keep the laughter in.

Eventually poor Ben realised that there was nothing for it but to walk home in his dirty shorts. He stomped across the nature reserve in the direction of our apartment. I almost succeeded in holding the laughter in, until he turned back and glared at me, saying: "And I suppose you think this is funny, do you?"

It was useless trying to stifle them any more – the giggles exploded out of me. Ben looked unimpressed and turned his back to carry on the stomp towards home, but this presented me with another view of his backside, which only made things seem even funnier. I laughed until my stomach ached.

Thankfully laughter is infectious and before long Ben began to see the funny side of the situation – at least he did until we reached the main road through the village. We had to follow this and cross a road bridge, which was thronged with cars and tourists on foot, before another couple of streets led us to the sanctuary of home. After a quick tactical debate, held with his back against a wall, we set off at a quick pace, with me trying my best to walk close enough behind Ben to hide the stain, but in reality probably just attracting more attention as we were walking in such a strange fashion.

We finally reached home and, after quickly dodging the neighbours, got Ben into the house and out of his muddy shorts. I felt bad about having laughed so much at his misfortune – but not so bad that I didn't instantly phone a friend to relay the whole debacle.

*

As peace descended after the frantic activity of summer, we had the chance to reflect once more on how our lives had changed since leaving England. We had spent nine months in

Portugal and had grown used to starting each day by having a drink on our sunny balcony. I definitely didn't miss spending mornings sitting in traffic on the A3, hating every other human being on the road while they made me late for work again. I also didn't miss having to use the train and tube on those days when I didn't use the car – instead the method of public transport I most commonly used in Portugal was the small boats that spent the summer ferrying passengers across the river to the island beaches and back.

Our diet had definitely changed for the better. Meals were cooked outside on the barbecue and we had time to sit and eat our sardine lunch in the sun, rather than grabbing a pastry while dashing from one part of London to another. The change in diet, as well as the increased exercise that a summer of almost daily swimming had provided, meant that we looked tanned and healthy, rather than pale and anaemic.

Whether because of the heat or because we had more time in our lives, we had both slowed down to a more relaxed pace. Although still capable of working hard, we had learned to combine this with enjoying more calming pursuits at the end of the working day, such as paddling in the waves or strolling along cobbled streets admiring the gently crumbling architecture.

There were down-sides to our new life too – or at least, there were things that we would have viewed as such when we lived in London. We had a lot less money, for example. This wasn't actually a problem, as our changed lifestyle meant that we didn't need as much money, but it was still a difficult thing to get used to. Having come from such a materialistic culture, perhaps this was not surprising. And despite the fact that our new life in the sunshine meant that we were less wealthy, we were so much happier and healthier that it was a trade we were both keen to accept.

Of course, that didn't mean we never had our doubtful moments.

Wobbles

Despite the sunshine, sand and sea, we occasionally had wobbly days about whether we had done the right thing by moving to Portugal. The fight to obtain our *residência* had brought about quite a few. Most expats we spoke to knew what we meant and had experienced the same uncertainties themselves from time to time.

Our efforts to learn Portuguese had started months before we made the move and I had studied for anywhere from ten minutes to an hour, four or five days each week, since we arrived. However, at the start of September it seemed that the Portuguese suddenly decided that everything we said was utterly incomprehensible. Maybe it was because they had spent the last three months speaking English to tourists, but practically everyone we interacted with ignored our efforts and insisted on speaking back to us in slow, condescending English.

Usually this language-based game was a source of entertainment for us. We have nicknamed it "the fight" and it can be played in shops, restaurants and various other locations. First we go in and speak Portuguese, then the Portuguese person replies in English. Everyone sticks to their guns until one party eventually gives in. If we give in and speak English, we lose the fight; if the Portuguese person ends up switching to Portuguese, we win.

That first week in September was really frustrating – we lost the game again and again. It made us feel that even years from now when we would (hopefully) be fluent, we would still be viewed as English people who couldn't possibly manage a whole conversation in Portuguese. After all the hours of studying and practice, this smarted quite a bit.

I also made a rather large conversational blunder while in a local bar, which further knocked my confidence. We had been having a couple of glasses of wine with some *petiscos* (the Portuguese version of tapas) and were nearly ready to leave when the owner delivered a plate of some delicious-smelling lamb to a lady sitting at the end of the bar.

"I would like to have that please," I said as he returned to where we were seated, pointing at the plate of food that the lady was tucking in to.

"One of those?" He chuckled.

"Yes. I would like to have that please."

The owner chuckled again, as did the lady at the end of the bar and the handful of other customers. Confused, I repeated my request a third time. More laughter.

I was halfway through repeating myself for the fourth time when I realised my mistake. My clumsy phrasing meant that instead of saying I wanted the dish that the woman was eating, I was asking for the woman herself. Cheeks flaming, I lowered my head and let Ben take care of the rest of the ordering that night.

*

Tackling our next Portuguese challenge – buying a car – had to be discussed at the start of September. We had been hiring cars as and when needed, usually when friends and family came to visit, then using our bikes the rest of the time. But we knew that eventually we would need to buy a car of our own and stop giving such large sums of cash to the hire car companies.

Ben had researched car prices in Portugal before we moved and we knew they were significantly higher than in England. We had debated taking our English car to Portugal, but the tales of woe regarding matriculation paperwork we had read on the expat forums, along with the cost of matriculation, had led us to decide against it. The horrors of the *residência* paperwork confirmed that this was the right decision.

But now the time had come to buy a car. We had prepared for the fact that the cost was going to be extortionate, but what we hadn't thought about was the actual process of the purchase. We knew nothing about cars – they held no interest for us other than as a means to get from A to B – and now we had to visit garages and try to ask the right questions in Portuguese, when we weren't even sure what we should have been asking in English.

Another wobbly day ensued. Finally we gave in and hired another car, negotiating a deal with the hire car company whereby we could do a five-month winter hire for a base-rate price. Not the ideal solution, but at least it meant that we didn't have to deal with purchasing a car until several months down the line.

Family and friends

Mid-September brought with it some exciting news – my mother and step-family had successfully purchased a property half an hour away from our apartment and were due to undertake a several-staged move starting in October. Soon we would have family just a short drive away. Excitedly we began planning which beaches we would show them first and which were the best restaurants to introduce them to.

We had also begun to make proper friends in our local area. A Portuguese couple of our own age had moved into one of the ground floor flats in our block with their young daughter. They were friendly and we always said hello when passing in the hallway or street.

One evening, Ben and I had a long barbecue planned. We barbecued a *salmonete* (sea trout) initially, then turned the gas down low to keep the barbecue warm while we ate, ready to cook the meat course next. Halfway through our fish, our neighbour rang the doorbell. He explained that he had seen a lot of smoke coming from our balcony and just wanted to check things were ok. We assured him that it was fine and that we had been barbecuing some fish, hence the smoke.

Although certain that all was well, we went to check the barbecue, just in case. As soon as we opened the balcony door we knew something was wrong. Huge clouds of smoke were billowing out of the barbecue and when Ben opened the lid flames roared up almost as high as his head. He quickly switched the gas off while I threw a bucketful of water over the flames. Disaster had been averted, thanks to our friendly neighbour.

The next day, we baked some cookies and took them downstairs, explaining that there had been a fire and that thanks to Mario the consequences had not been major. The day after, Mario came up to return the cookie plate, complete with a still-warm cake, which his wife Andrea had baked to thank us for the cookies. And thus a tradition was born – we began regularly swapping food gifts back and forth and would stop for longer chats in the street or when we were all in the pool together. Portuguese people are slower to make friends than English people, but when they do, they embrace you into their lives.

We had also befriended a young English couple who lived and worked in our local area and whom we had met a few times while out on the town that summer. Hard-working, fun-loving and very much on our wavelength, they filled a gap in our lives which we hadn't really noticed was there.

After our wobbles earlier in the month, we finally felt that we were putting down roots.

*

Another barbecue-related accident followed shortly after the fire. We had spent the afternoon at my mum's new property in the countryside, exploring the orchard and raiding the plentiful fruit trees. I had gathered a delightful basketful of bounty, revelling in the fresh air, exercise and sweet-smelling trees.

That evening, we settled down for a barbecue and a couple of glasses of wine. Mum and I descaled the sardines and Ben volunteered to cook them. All went well until we ran out of charcoal. There wasn't enough heat left to cook the last of the sardines, but Ben was not to be deterred. Mum's house had an outdoor kitchen complete with gas hob, so Ben grabbed a frying pan and decided to experiment with frying the last few fish.

Mum and I were sitting and chatting when suddenly we heard a loud yell followed by a string of expletives – hardly the kind of language Ben would usually use in front of his mother-in-law. We dashed over to see what was wrong.

Ben was running his hand under the outdoor tap (thankfully right next to the hob), his face white under his tan. While he had been turning the sardines over in the frying pan, he had somehow knocked its handle and tipped the fish and a fair quantity of sizzling oil directly onto his hand.

The pain was enormous – Ben couldn't take his hand out from under the water for more than two seconds before he had to plunge it back in. He kept it there for several minutes, while mum and I flitted around him, unsure of what to do to help.

One thing Ben has always been afraid of is medical issues – even talking about anything medical makes him feel woozy. With mum and I debating what more you could do for burns than run them under cold water, Ben began to sway. Luckily I saw him do it and promptly ordered him to lie on the floor. He did as instructed and while I held his legs above the level of his heart (at least I remembered what to do for people who feel faint!), mum filled a bucket of water for him to put his hand in.

Gradually the colour began to return to his face and he felt stable enough to stand, but the pain in his hand was still intense. After a further 15 minutes under the tap, he moved on to a bowl of ice water. (I have since learned that this is not how burns should be treated, as it can actually make them worse, but I didn't know any better at the time.) Within minutes of Ben's hand going into the ice water, the heat from his hand had turned it tepid.

Mum and I kept up a flow of fresh ice water bowls until about 1 am, when Ben finally felt up to heading home. We filled a bowl for the car ride and I drove back to our apartment, settling him on the sofa bed in front of a film. His medical phobia was such that any thought of having his burn treated in hospital was ruled out.

I sat up, surreptitiously consulting the internet to find out what the signs of shock were and keeping an eye on Ben, until about 4 am when he finally began to doze off – through sheer exhaustion rather than any real abatement of the pain. He managed to fall asleep with his hand still in the bowl of water and I too began to nod off from my position on the other sofa.

Just as I was dropping off, I saw Ben twitch in his sleep. He must have had an itchy face, as he pulled his burned hand out of the water in order to scratch his cheek. In doing so he managed to wake himself up by trailing cold water all over his face, providing the evening's only light relief.

The next morning, three of Ben's fingers had swelled to the size of thick English sausages. They were bright purple-red and covered in giant blisters. I went to the pharmacy as soon as it was open and bought the ointments and bandages that they recommended for burns, then went home to do my best at nursing.

It took several days for the swelling to go down and for the blisters to shrink and then burst (a highly unpleasant moment). Poor Ben had to bathe with his bandaged hand wrapped in a carrier bag for over a week in order to protect his fingers as they began to heal. It was several weeks before they healed fully, but eventually his skin returned to almost normal colour.

*

While Ben was still healing, our niece Amy arrived, fleeing

the English late summer rain and joining us for some sunny beach days. We did more touristy things, including going on a banana boat (which I loved, but Ben hated) and going ocean kayaking.

The kayaking was Amy's idea – she is somewhat more active than we are – but it sounded like fun so we booked to go on a day trip, which included lunch on a deserted island. We arrived a few minutes late (which for us, with our legendarily poor timekeeping, was actually pretty good), to find about 12 other sporty types already in their life jackets and being assigned their boats. We were given life jackets and paddles, then a quick demonstration of how to use them. The instructor asked if there was anyone present who hadn't kayaked before. We duly put up our hands – the only three in the group to do so. The instructor didn't look pleased.

The plan for the day was a morning of kayaking, with a quick stop for swimming, followed by more kayaking out to a stunning deserted island for lunch, beer and snorkelling. Then an afternoon of kayaking back to where we started. It sounded like great fun and, for Ben and Amy, it was (despite Ben repeatedly banging his still-raw fingers on the side of the kayak).

Sadly, for me, the kayaking did not go well. I was useless at it. Within minutes of us all setting out, the rest of the group were just specks in the distance, while I struggled with my paddle and got nowhere fast. I persevered, but got caught in some kind of tide that took me round in circles. After three laps of struggling and still ending up back in the same place I had had enough. The water was only waist deep, so I jumped out, thumped the stupid kayak and then dragged it after me while I waded towards where the others had disappeared.

After calming down a few minutes later, I got back in the kayak and tried again. I was, unsurprisingly, still terrible at it. The instructor came back to find out what had happened to me. Seeing my inability to get anywhere, he promptly tied me to the support boat and left me tethered there for the rest of the day, like a naughty child. I then had to endure the humiliation of being dragged past the rest of my group, who all found it most entertaining. At least the lunch and snorkelling were good.

In fairness, Ben and Amy both really enjoyed the kayaking and said it was something they would like to do again. I will not be joining them when they do.

Nearly there

It was hard to believe, but as October brought with it some slight relief from the ferocious heat of summer, we realised that we had been living in Portugal for nearly a year. The time seemed to have flown by in a wonderful whirlwind of barbecues, beaches and wine. Thinking back over our past almost-year, despite the occasional wobble and the fact that it had not all been plain sailing, we had no regrets about making the move.

We had experienced first-hand all of the different seasons and had lived so many new and exciting experiences. We still had many "firsts" to come, some less pleasant than others, such as going through the process of buying our first car or completing our first tax returns, but began to realise how far we had come already and how we had changed in the process. We no longer felt the need to live life at breakneck pace. We walked more slowly, taking in our surroundings and enjoying where we lived. We spent longer over meals – both over the cooking and the eating of them. We scaled and gutted fish and chopped the necks and heads off chickens without batting an eyelid. We sucked the heads of prawns when presented with them in restaurants.

Our family members moving to Portugal emphasised how much we had learned. They had a lot of questions, most of which we knew the answer to, even though it had felt at times that we hadn't learned that much!

Our Portuguese had come on well too – we could now catch some of the meaning of news stories on the radio and understand a little of the conversations going on around us in restaurants and cafés. We were far from fluent, but had made so much progress compared to our first stuttered attempts at speaking a year ago.

We had also put on weight – a summer of eating seafood in rich, buttery sauces and drinking caipirinhas with two table-spoonfuls of sugar in each had taken its toll. The caipirinha is Brazil's national cocktail and is available in bars all over the Algarve. It's made with cachaça (sugar cane rum), plus plenty of sugar, fresh lime and crushed ice. It's both potent and refreshing, but also sadly very fattening. It was time to tackle the weight we had gained, so we started WeightWatchers and began to exercise.

Exercise is something that never really appealed to me in London. Somehow, after the commute to and from work, plus the actual day at work, I didn't really have the energy to do much other than potter around the house and make dinner. I have never been sure whether to be awed or bemused by those Londoners who don their Lycra in all weathers to pound the pavements or head to the gym.

I was still busy in Portugal, but the lack of commute meant that I had two hours more free time each day than I had had in England. With my weight creeping up, I decided to start running.

My first week of running was hard. I started gently, running (well, half jogging and half walking) for 20 minutes before work two days in a row. By Wednesday my legs were so stiff that I could barely move. I rested for a day, then pushed on with the regime for the following two days, much to Ben's amuse-ment as I limped my way stiff-legged around the apartment.

The second week was easier. I began to pick up speed and my muscles began to get used to actually having to do something strenuous for a change. I would run down to the seafront and then along the boardwalk, watching the sunrise turn the water pink and orange while the boats bobbed around in it.

Each day my stamina increased a little more and soon I could run for an hour or more before starting to feel the strain. It was a new part to my life that I embraced wholeheartedly. Running across the nature reserve, I saw wild flamingoes feeding in the early morning light. By the seafront, I saw fishermen moving their craft along the coast, a trail of squawking seagulls trailing behind them. (Less inspiring sites included some off-season tourists reeling along the street after drinking all night, and two dogs copulating in a park.) Each run was different and some were harder than others, but every single one of them beat sitting in a car on the A3. I had found another thing to love and be thankful for about our life in Portugal.

Christmas is coming around again

By November, the new regime of WeightWatchers and running had quickly dealt with the weight problem and gave us a chance to enjoy more of the fresh, locally grown fruit, vegetables and salad leaves available from the market. The exercise was something we would never have found time for back in London, but in Portugal runs along the seafront before work in the morning, as the sun rose and turned the water golden, quickly became a much-loved part of my daily routine.

The start of November meant that we had now lived in Portugal for a whole year – and what a whirlwind it had been since we stepped onto that plane at Gatwick. It had been without question one of the most eventful years of our lives, but we barely had time to mark the occasion, what with another work trip back to England and preparations for our second Christmas in Portugal.

We decided to save a few euros at Christmas and learn from the mistakes of the previous year. Rather than buying expensive imported cranberry sauce (€3) and mincemeat (€5) in Portugal, we happily toured an English supermarket during our UK work trip in early December, filling our case with cost-saving delicacies.

Sadly, our enthusiasm for English Christmas products – combined with a certain budget airline's decision to reduce travellers' baggage allowances –scuppered our thrifty plans.

After we had paid our overweight baggage charge at Gatwick, we returned to Portugal having paid far more for the Christmas items than if we had just purchased them in Portugal in the first place.

We didn't let it affect our Christmas spirit. The day after we got back we were off to the Christmas market at the beautiful hamlet of Cacela Velha – a collection of picture-perfect little cottages set on a cliff-top, nestled around a pretty church overlooking the sea.

The market was a delight – a collection of stalls selling local handicrafts, cakes, jams, plants and wine. We indulged in artisan quiches and sticky honey pastries (WeightWatchers was already long forgotten) while we strolled around in the bright December sunshine. We also sampled local wines and purchased a number of Christmas treats for ourselves and our nearest and dearest.

After the market, we drove along the coast to the border town of Vila Real de Santo Antonio for more strolling, eating and Christmas gift-purchasing. I spent a delightful 20 minutes in a shop dedicated solely to the sale of festive decorations, until Ben finally managed to drag me away, my bags bulging with baubles, nativity tea-light scenes and strings of sparkly tinsel.

In the centre of the town we came across a real treat – a huge model village constructed especially for Christmas and free to enter. Thousands of little figures nestled in a vast range of scenes, with moving parts and lights completing the effect. Tourists and locals alike wandered around the display, pointing out its features and taking photographs. From babes in arms to a rather elderly party of nuns, everyone seemed enchanted with the scenes laid out before them.

When we had finally seen enough, we headed off to a nearby café for a revitalising cup of coffee and sweet *pastel de nata* before returning home, full of Christmas spirit and ready to find places for all of our new Christmas purchases in our apartment.

With the arrival of the Christmas holidays, the usual drinking and dining began in earnest. We combined English traditions with Portuguese ones, particularly where food and drink were concerned. On Christmas Eve we had our traditional buffet style feast, only this year it consisted of a myriad of fresh shellfish caught in our local sea. We baked biscuits and breads and made chutneys, but all with local ingredients that made them stand out from our usual English fare.

Ben's mother, her partner and his mother flew to see us for a few days over Christmas. Diana conquered her 40-year fear of flying to do so, which delighted us and made Christmas extra special as we introduced various members of our extended and blended family to each other.

So we drank and ate, and drank some more, opened our gifts, ate and drank even more and then suddenly it was Boxing Day and the festivities had passed for another year. Sad though the thought was, the sun was shining and the day called for an outing, so we headed up to show Ben's family the view at Cacela Velha, looking out over the sea as the sun sparkles danced across it. The little church was open and full of people dressed in their best, and we took the time to admire the beautiful interior before walking to a nearby restaurant to share a couple of plates of clams. That evening Ben was complaining of having sore skin on his face and neck – upon examination we realised that he had managed to get sunburned on Boxing Day! We wondered at the variety of Portuguese winter: last year we had been shivering in a mouldy, leaking house as the seemingly endless rain poured down; this year the sun had been as hot as mid-summer in England. At times we felt we would never get used to our new country.

Taking on the world

As the weeks rolled by in the new year, it was time to tackle some more Portuguese paperwork. Although we had struck our deal with a local hire car company, the agreed period was coming to an end and our trusty little hire car had to go back. After that, we knew the price would rise swiftly as the tourists started flocking to the Algarve as things geared up for another season. It was time to buy a car of our own.

Tax on cars in Portugal has driven up prices to way beyond the English rates we were used to. Most Portuguese people tackle this by taking out a long-term loan in order to purchase their cars – in much the same way as people in the UK take out mortgages to purchase their houses.

We resisted the idea of a loan at first, instead looking at what we could get for our money. We only wanted a little run-around to go to the shops, the beach and the airport. In England, we could have spent £750 and got something that would have lasted a year or so. In Portugal, our €5,000 was just enough to buy an unreliable old banger. After looking at several cars with faded upholstery, tape decks and unusual odours, we decided it was time to apply for a loan.

Our bank told us that getting a loan would not be a problem. We just had to complete some forms and provide proof of income. The local branch would then send this to London for verification, after which the loan would be ours. It sounded straightforward enough, so we signed on the dotted line and then waited the required two weeks, meanwhile spending countless hours looking at car reviews online.

After the two weeks was up, we went back to the bank.

"I'm sorry, but the paperwork is not yet back from England," said the kindly assistant. "It will be perhaps one more week."

We waited another week then went back to the bank, only to be told the same thing. Meanwhile, the global economy was crumbling all around us and we read frequent reports in the papers about how hard it was becoming to be accepted for loans. We began to worry.

After another week, the bank called us to say that our paperwork had been returned from England and we could now apply for our loan. They assured us that this was just a formality so, with the usual huge folder of paperwork, we went in and signed the necessary forms.

A week went by, then two. We had to extend our hire car booking, paying significantly more for March's rental than we had for the previous month. Every time I phoned the bank, they said that our application was being processed and we would have the loan soon.

Finally the bank called.

"We're very sorry, but your loan is not approved. The bank is not making any loans at the moment because of the economic problems." I could hear a warranty-less, no-service-history banger calling to us.

We still had one option available to us – car finance from a main dealer. We once more gathered up the enormous paperwork folder and began touring car dealerships in Faro. This is something I don't enjoy at all. To me, one car looks exactly the same as another – the only way I can tell them apart is the colour. Thankfully, we found the car we wanted in only the second garage we went to.

I chatted to the saleswoman in Portuguese (she didn't speak any English) and explained to her that we wanted to buy a car on finance. I brandished my huge document folder and she took us into her office. We began filling out forms and passing her documents. Unfortunately, one of the things which we didn't routinely carry around in our document folder was our wage slips. The omission brought the whole process to a halt. We returned home, but bright and early the next day we went back to the car dealership, armed with wage slips and every other document we could think of. The saleswoman slowly piled them up, ticking off a list in front of her. We filled out the finance application form and she took that from us too. The whole process had taken nearly two hours. Getting up with her mountain of paperwork, she began to head over to the photocopier. Suddenly she paused and turned back to us.

"How long have you lived in Portugal?"

"About 18 months," I replied.

"Oh – in that case you will probably need a Portuguese guarantor for your loan."

"I'm sorry?" My heart sank. I hoped desperately that I had misunderstood.

"Someone Portuguese who can be your guarantor. For your loan."

"But we don't have anyone here who can do that – my parents could do it, but they're English."

"Oh." She looked confused for a moment. "Well, in that case we can still put the application in for you, but I don't think it will be successful."

Having dropped her bombshell, the saleswoman turned on her heel and headed off to undertake the task of photocopying our reams of paperwork: a seemingly futile task after her parting comment.

On the way home we stopped to look at some more old bangers. I could have cried with frustration.

A week later, having heard nothing from the car dealership, we had given up all hope of getting a loan. We were shopping in Faro, just a few minutes away from our much-longed-for car, when my mobile rang. It was the saleswoman.

"I have good news for you – your loan has been approved!"

I asked her to repeat what she had just said, not quite able to believe that our luck had turned and the car saga might be close to a conclusion.

"It is good news – you have the loan. You can come and sign the paperwork for your car."

Five minutes later we were in her office, signing yet more forms. It would be a couple more weeks until the car was officially ours, but there were no more hurdles in the way.

Two weeks later we went to collect our car. It not only symbolised our triumph over bureaucracy, but meant that we had finally purchased something that confirmed our long-term commitment to life in our new country. We were both smiling as we drove away from the garage.

Paying our dues

In tandem with the "buying a car" saga, we had to tackle the issue of completing our first Portuguese tax return. Thanks to yet more Internet research, Ben had established that we needed to pay our taxes in Portugal (despite earning our money in England), as we were now fiscally resident there.

We went to see Accountant Number One in January. He spent an hour looking over our documents, before advising us that we should just continue to pay our tax in England; if we paid it in Portugal, it would cost us more. We spent the next half hour explaining that we were intending to live in Portugal long-term and that our research had shown that we were obliged to pay our taxes here. He shrugged, muttering about "grey areas". We left his office feeling less than confident.

A week later, we received a bill from his firm for twice what we had been told we would be charged. Upon querying it, we were told that the price had been doubled as there were two of us. We argued our case, provided proof of what we had been quoted, paid the firm for one hour and started looking for another accountant.

Accountant Number Two seemed a little more promising. We met with him and gave him some of our paperwork. He advised us to pay our tax in England as it would cost us less, but then seemed to accept that we wanted to adhere to the letter of the law and pay it in Portugal. We left him with a few queries and followed up with emails, to which he did not respond. After four weeks of silence, I arranged another meeting with him via his secretary.

Accountant Number Two arrived 45 minutes late for our second meeting. Although I forgive Ben's persistent tardiness, I am a huge fan of punctuality and was far from impressed. We were ushered into his office, where he proceeded to reveal that he had done nothing since our last meeting, other than lose the documents we had left with him. Then he shrugged and suggested we just continue to pay our taxes in England. We began the search for Accountant Number Three.

*

In addition to the frustration of dealing with Portuguese accountants, I had the additional task of having to deal with HMRC in England to arrange for my wages to be paid gross so that I could pay my tax in Portugal. I had filled out the necessary forms and posted them at the start of January. I phoned to confirm they received my letter, but was told that they were behind with opening their post and that they hoped to get to my letter by mid-February.

I phoned HMRC again at the end of February, to be told that the target date for opening my letter was now early March. I began to panic – if this wasn't sorted before the end of March, I would be unlikely to receive the English rebate before my tax had to be paid in Portugal, and I needed the rebate from England in order to afford my Portuguese tax bill.

Finally, on 14th March I received confirmation that my NT tax code had been applied. This meant we had overcome the first hurdle of being able to have the money in the right country when tax time came around. However, the delays and apathy of Accountants Numbers One and Two, combined with a two-week work trip to England, meant that it was not until early May that we found Accountant Number Three.

Accountant Number Three was clever. She was helpful. She knew the Portuguese and English tax and social security systems inside out. She listened as we explained our situation in detail and then told us exactly what we needed to do. Everything she said tallied with our research and she confirmed that we should be paying our tax in Portugal. After an hour and a half with her, she asked for our signatures on a couple of forms. That was it – everything we had spent months trying to sort out was achieved in the space of a morning. It was all we could do not to declare our undying love for her on the spot.

Climbing Foia

Suddenly, with all of the car and tax paperwork sorted, we had free time again. A blissful three weeks of carefree sunny evenings and weekends followed. We visited beaches, ate clams sitting in the sunshine and generally enjoyed afresh everything that we had moved to the Algarve for in the first place.

A flurry of visitors gave us the excuse to revisit some of our favourite spots and many happy hours were spent bobbing around in the sea, despite its early year chilliness.

Another visit from our niece Amy (the one responsible for my kayaking humiliation), who was training for a challenge in England, involved slightly more active pursuits, including some delightful hikes along flower-scented cliffs. She also persuaded us (I'm not sure how) to climb Foia – the Algarve's highest mountain. Thus early one morning we set off for the western end of the Algarve, stopping to collect my mother on the way, as she also fancied a day of mountaineering.

Armed with our guide book and plentiful bottles of water in our backpacks, we headed for the delightful little town of Monchique, where our climb was to begin. Our first stop was a café on the town square, where we filled up on coffee and freshly baked pastries to give us additional energy for the climb. We sat in the sun as we ate and watched local children playing around the town's small fountain.

When we ran out of excuses to delay, we finally started the climb, winding our way up through the town along the path described in the guide book. Pretty, twisting streets and cob-bled steps shortly gave way to a wooded path. The sunlight streamed through the trees as we trekked upwards, pausing to catch our breath at a long-deserted (and, to my mind, rather creepy) tumbledown abbey.

As we continued upwards, the path became a little less clear, but we soldiered on and seemed to be heading in the right direction, judging by the occasional piece of red and white tape tied to a tree, which it seemed other walkers had left as guides.

We crossed a road and carried on upwards, eventually leav-ing the woods and coming out on a shelterless trail up the side of the mountain. Here we encountered pretty flowers by the wayside, as well as stunning views over the surrounding countryside. We also, unfortunately, encountered some rather persistent bees. They took a particular liking to Ben who, when he saw they were not going to leave him alone, bolted up the mountain in an effort to shake them off. Needless to say, he tired before the bees did. Shouting up the mountain to him, we let him know that it looked as if it was his T-shirt they were particularly interested in. He promptly pulled it off and threw it on the path, stamping his foot and having a mini temper tantrum, much to the amusement of the rest of us. The bees buzzed happily around Ben's discarded T-shirt, while my poor hot, tired husband trudged a little further up the trail to sit down and sulk. We followed him up the mountain, retrieving his T-shirt on the way, and after a couple of steep switchbacks in the path, the bees lost interest and we were able to continue without further harassment.

The trail became steeper and steeper, but we persevered. The sun was beating down on our unprotected heads, with the day fulfilling its 28°C promise. As we reached a smaller trail, off to our right, we paused for a drink. I sat on a rock to catch my breath. As I sat, I noticed my feet begin to tingle strangely. Then my hands began to do the same and I could hear a strange low buzzing noise. Thankfully my mum spotted I was about to pass out before things went any further and gave me a big bottle of water. Along with some of my niece's jelly babies, this did the trick and after a few minutes of rest we continued upwards.

The final part of the journey – along a small road winding around the top of Foia – afforded us some amazing views, as the land rolled away to the side of us. Tiny sheep grazed in the fields below, the gentle tinkling of their bells just reaching us on the quickening breeze.

Some minutes later, we reached the summit. Barely registering the spectacular views, we headed straight for the café, where we guzzled down glass after glass of iced tea and treated ourselves to ice creams. Once refreshed, we admired the view and took some pictures, before visiting the gift shop (the part of the day that Amy had been most excited about) to purchase some little reminders of our visit.

We followed the same trail for our descent, but had walked only a short way before grey clouds came rolling in. As is common for mountainous regions, the weather turned quickly and soon fat rain drops were splashing down on us as we walked. The occasional crack of thunder and the increasing ferocity of the rain encouraged us to walk fast, but were also a welcome relief from the relentless heat we had encountered on the way up. As we once more entered the woods, the rain storm passed and we emerged back in Monchique in glorious sunshine. After a celebratory beer, we headed back home. Our feet ached and we were damp and tired, but all of us felt a great sense of achievement at having climbed the Algarve's highest mountain.

After another few days of holiday, our niece returned home

to England. She was the last of our flurry of guests to depart, which meant it was once more time to start focusing on the dreaded paperwork.

The *câmara*

Towards the end of May, I began work on renewing our *residência*. We had originally been granted *residência* for only a year, instead of the usual five (seemingly for no reason in particular), and all too soon the end of that year was approaching. Remembering the farcical and lengthy process the year before, I determined to start early.

Both the EU website and the SEF (Portuguese immigration authority) website stated that all I needed to do was take my passport to the SEF office and sign a form to say that I was able to support myself. The SEF would then give me a five-year temporary residency document, which after five years would be exchanged for a permanent residency document. Simple.

Having been resident for nearly a year, paid taxes and bought a car, I felt settled in Portugal and confident in my right to live and work there. Paperwork in hand, I entered the *câmara* with my head held high.

I was served by the same lady who had dealt with me the year before. Ignoring this ill omen, I presented my request for a five year *residência* certificate for myself and my husband. The lady produced a form and ticked off a list of documents that would be required – passport (check), proof of address (check), employment contract (check), passport photograph (check) and social security number (oh dear).

I handed over the documents I had, hoping that they would suffice. The lady looked at my employment contract and shook her head.

"This must be in Portuguese."

"But I work for an English company and so my contract is in English."

"This must be in Portuguese."

I wrote "translate employment contract into Portuguese" on my To Do list.

I then explained that my husband didn't have an employment contract as he was self-employed and ran his own business. I produced a copy of our tax return to show this. The lady glanced at it and then pushed it back across the counter, entirely uninterested in the fact that our payment of a five-figure sum to the Portuguese government was fairly concrete proof that we earned enough to support ourselves financially in Portugal. Apparently only a contract of employment would do. I wrote "tell Ben to write himself a contract of employment with his own company" on the To Do list, then added "plus translate it into Portuguese".

Next, we turned to the social security issue. In my best Portuguese, I explained that it was not possible for me to have a social security number. In Portugal, social security numbers can be issued if you are a) employed by a Portuguese company, or b) self-employed. I was neither and explained this to the lady in the *câmara*. She shook her head and advised that we both needed to obtain a *declaracao da segurança social com os descontos efectuados* – a formal statement from the social security office that we didn't owe the government any social security payments. After circling round the same conversation a few times, I despondently returned home.

My next move was to contact our accountant to discuss the social security problem. She recommended a document agency, but the previously unhelpful encounter with such an agency had made us wary. Instead, we resorted to even more Internet research. This led to a new plan and the next day, documents in hand, we walked through town to the SEF office.

We showed the SEF lady our documents and a print-out from the SEF website (dated the previous month) stating that all we had to do was show our passports and sign a form in order to obtain our *residência*. The lady at the SEF informed us that the law had been changed four years previously. We asked why their website had not been updated to reflect this. The lady shrugged and we returned home, empty-handed and annoyed.

Our last hope was to recruit a lawyer. I met with one in our local town who came recommended. After running through the details of our case, she advised the best course of action was to visit the social security office to try to obtain the form the *câmara* was demanding. I explained that they would not give me such a form without a social security number, but agreed it was worth a try.

Later that week, I arrived at the social security office, where the lawyer was due to meet me. Together we spoke with an advisor, who explained that it was not possible to issue me with either a social security number or the required form. She confirmed that there was no mechanism available in Portugal by which someone in my situation could pay social security and that I should continue to pay National Insurance in the UK, as there was an EU reciprocal agreement in place to cover situations such as this. Unfortunately, the EU reciprocal agreement was not in any way able to help me get hold of the form I needed for the *câmara*.

Time was rapidly running out – we had only one week to go before our original *residência* expired. This meant that unless we somehow got the paperwork sorted, we would technically become illegal immigrants in eight days' time, something neither of us was prepared to do. While I sat and cried in the lawyer's office, Ben began looking at property for rent just across the Spanish border.

*

The following day I was back in the lawyer's office. She had prepared a power of attorney document that would allow her to liaise with the *câmara* on our behalf. It required both our signatures, but Ben was at home working, so I trekked back to the apartment, obtained his autograph and then returned the document to the lawyer.

Actual progress was made the next day – our lawyer phoned to say she had persuaded the *câmara* to drop the requirement for the social security declaration form. Instead, they would accept three months' worth of bank statements from us, along with my translated contract of employment. We began to dare to hope.

The bad news was that the *câmara* would not accept our application until the day after our current one ran out, meaning that we would technically be illegally staying in the country while our application was processed. However, the lawyer assured us that we should be able to obtain a stamped form showing that our application was under way, which would at least demonstrate that we were attempting to renew our *residência*.

*

The big day finally came. We headed back to the *câmara*, lawyer and documents all at hand. I had paid the lawyer to translate my employment contract, so put this on the counter first. The lady in the *câmara* glanced at it.

"I do not need this," she said, pushing it back towards me.

She was, however, interested in our bank statements and

had a good, long look at them. Then she asked for proof that we were covered for medical treatment. This had not been mentioned at any point before now. In a rare piece of paper-work-related good fortune, we both had our private medical insurance cards in our wallets. She scooped these up, along with our numerous other documents and went to photocopy the lot. We began to get excited – had we finally done it?

Sadly, we hadn't. The *câmara* lady returned our original documents to us, stamped our forms, then told us to come back in a week. At least she stamped the forms we needed to allow us to stay in the country while our application was being processed.

*

Five nights of broken sleep and anxious waiting later, it was Ben's birthday. We weren't due to hear from the *câmara* until the following day, but I secretly arranged for the lawyer to pop to the *câmara* and check to see if our documents had by some miracle been processed early. An hour later, she emailed me a copy of two shiny new residency certificates. I don't think Ben has ever been more delighted with a birthday gift!

Oranges

The property that my mother and step-family had bought, just half an hour's drive from our village, was very different from our modern apartment. It was a sprawling set of interconnected houses and outbuildings, surround by acres of orange trees and interspersed with plums, apples, persimmons, pomegranates, pears and even the odd rambling grape vine. It came with its own well, rusty tractor, curious faulty electrics and an unmovable German tenant. The houses needed some work, but everyone was up for the challenge.

The family was also enthusiastic (to varying degrees) about the idea of becoming orange farmers. The outgoing owners of the property had agreed to help with the arrangements for the first year's harvest. As the oranges swelled to their sweet, juicy peak, mum set to work making every orange-based recipe under the sun, and still there were tens of thousands of oranges left dangling from the branches.

When official harvest time arrived, the outgoing owners arranged for the picking crew to deliver the crates, then provide two days of labour to get all the oranges picked and packed. On day one, mum got up early and tramped out into the orchard. Starting at one corner, she began happily picking oranges. She had filled about five crates when a Portuguese man came dashing through the orchard.

"No! It is all wrong!" He was the first of the picking crew

to arrive and swiftly proceeded to show her in just how many ways she had picked and packed the oranges wrongly – it turned out there was a lot more to harvesting oranges than just pulling them off the tree and putting them in boxes.

After a rather stern lesson and with the rest of the picking crew arriving promptly only 30 minutes behind schedule, the harvest began in earnest. After a tiring day, just over half the trees had been stripped of their fruit.

The next day, mum was up early again. She had to go into Faro to sort out some paperwork for the day (a common activity for most expats in Portugal), but before she left she tied a number of red ribbons around the trunks of selected trees – these were the oranges that were to be left for the family's use. When the pickers arrived, mum explained the system. They set to work on the non-marked trees and she left them to it.

By the time mum returned home that evening, the picking crew and their crates full of oranges had disappeared. It seemed strange to see the trees without their brightly coloured oranges on, as though the orchard had suddenly gone bald. Upon investigation, mum realised that the orchard had gone a little too bald – despite the carefully marked trees, not a single orange was left. The pickers had taken the lot. In the course of two days the family had gone from having more oranges than they could count, to needing to buy them from the local store.

Caring for the trees had been hard work. The family had walked acre after acre, carefully checking each pipeline of the watering system and mending any leaks. They had invested in nutrients and fertilizer, as well as replacing the rusty tractor with a more serviceable model. Their crash course in citrus tree care had been intensive and expensive and, at the end of it all, they had been left with a cheque that just covered their costs and no oranges for their own use.

Despite all this, work to raise the next year's crop had to continue. Bay trees and olive bushes, which sprouted wild all over the orchard the second you turned your back, had to be dug out and removed to give the orange trees room to grow. Each orange tree had to be checked for signs of disease and the soil tested for its acidity and nutrient levels. The watering regime had to be readjusted to prepare for the fierce heat of summer.

The spirit in which the work was undertaken was, it has to be said, somewhat less enthusiastic than it had been when the family first bought the property. There were even some mutterings about cutting the whole lot down and having a huge orangey bonfire.

Ben and I did our best to remain enthusiastic and offer encouragement for the whole orange farming venture. Given that all we had to do was watch from a distance while others did the work, and we benefited from free oranges for several months of the year, this was not hard to do.

One hot evening after a hard day's work in the orchard (for the family), Ben and I popped round to cook a barbecue for the workers. It was a typically long Algarve feast, supplemented by a few glasses of vodka and freshly squeezed orange juice. I commented on how good the juice was, which prompted my step-uncle to turn to his father and say:

"Oh, that reminds me dad, can you put orange juice on the shopping list?"

It turned out that despite having access to the sweetest juice I've ever tasted, simply by walking into his back garden, my step-uncle was still buying cartons of expensive, acidic orange juice from his local shop.

Naturally, much teasing about his laziness ensued and both Ben and I got the giggles. When my mum came back from indoors a few minutes later, I relayed the shocking revelation to her, expecting her to find it as funny as I did, but she just stood there, looking like a rabbit caught in the headlights.

It was then that the whole sorry tale came out – all four of the wannabe orange farmers regularly bought cartons of orange juice at the store rather than stepping into their back garden, plucking ripe fruit from the trees and juicing it. Ben and I dissolved into laughter once more.

Losing our Englishness

With a routine work trip to England at the end of June came the sudden realisation that we were beginning to lose our Englishness – or at least our London-ness. We walked in to the hotel, cases in hand, and Ben greeted the staff with a loud *"Olá! Bom dia!"* Red-faced, he realised his error and left me to handle the check-in process.

It wasn't the last time we accidentally spoke Portuguese on that trip. It seemed that words like "hello" and "thank you" now came more naturally in Portuguese than in English, although we were both still far from fluent.

We noticed other subtle changes too. While queuing in the supermarket on my lunch break, I noticed that I was waiting patiently, rather than fuming about the loss of a few precious minutes. Amused by the change, I smiled at people in the street as I headed back to the office – then remembered as people scowled back at me that that wasn't the done thing in London!

Other things caught our attention. The noise of London's traffic and the smell of exhaust as we walked down the street were really noticeable, yet we hadn't even been aware of these during our life in England – they had just been part of a background that we took for granted. Now we craved a return to the quiet, fresh air of home, with its faintly salty sea smell.

The aggression displayed by drivers was also strange to us

now. In our sleepy village, blocking a one-way street by pulling up to chat to a friend you had spotted was entirely acceptable. The cars behind would wait patiently for a few minutes while you had a natter. In London the blaring horns and rude gestures when someone failed to pull away at a traffic light at the split-second it turned green provided quite a contrast.

Some things caught me by surprise. After dinner in the hotel one evening, I decided to do a spot of clothes shopping, until Ben pointed out that all the shops closed at 6 pm. At home we were used to everything being open until at least 11 pm, so we ran on a later timetable there. It was not unusual for the barbecue to be lit just as midnight was approaching.

Ben claimed that his timekeeping had become Portuguese, as he now wasn't worried about being late for appointments. Given that he had never been on time for anything since I had known him (other than our wedding) I suspected this was more of a justification of his tardiness rather than a genuine Portugal-induced change.

We had begun to crave Portuguese food while in England. After two days of filling up on things we couldn't get at home (mainly sausage rolls, taramasalata and pad thai), we suddenly found ourselves wanting *bacalhau à brás* and *arroz de pato* for dinner. We compromised and had piri-piri chicken from Nando's.

The weather was something we really noticed. Friends we met up with were in shorts, T-shirts and summer dresses, enjoying the 27°C heat. I was in jeans and wishing I'd thought to bring a thicker cardigan to England with me.

Silly little things caught our attention too. Ben remarked on how strangely large £20 notes now felt. I was amused by how unusual it felt to stand on carpet in the hotel rather than on the now more familiar tiled floors.

After 20 months of life in Portugal, the country and its customs – even its language, to a certain extent – had truly begun to take hold of us. That particular trip back to England helped us to recognise just how much we had become accustomed to our new way of life. We still had a lot to learn, but it was good to know how far we had already come. We might have begun to lose some of our Englishness, but it was more than compensated for by the Portuguese-ness that was replacing it.

*

Catching up with friends in London was good, but we had begun to dread the inevitable question "So, how's Portugal?" The reality was that life for everyone in Portugal was getting harder as the world economy stumbled. This included us, but no matter what we said, friends seemed to think that we spent all day floating in the pool and drinking cocktails.

This was far from the reality of the situation. We both worked fulltime and things like the weekly shop and housework had not vanished from our lives simply because we had moved to another country. When friends came to stay from England, we took leave from work and spent the days lounging on the beach and barbecuing. They went back home with the impression that this was how we spent our lives.

No matter what we said, sympathy was not forthcoming. Our routine meant that by the time work was done, the sun had lost much of its strength. We were less tanned after nearly two years of living in Portugal than most of the tourists we encountered wandering around our village. The closest we got to the pool most days was listening to the sounds of holiday-makers splashing around, while we sat inside typing. By the time the working week was over, the apartment would need cleaning, the shopping needed to be done and all those chores we had put off during the week had to be tackled. Usually it was Sunday afternoon before we found time to think about trying to grab a couple of hours outside – much like life in England!

Portugal's worsening economic situation was having an effect too. Bills were getting bigger and money tighter. New tax measures meant that we would have to pay an extra 3.5% on our earnings that year, when we were already on a significantly higher tax rate than we had been in the UK. Just like our friends "back home" we were tightening our belts and doing our best to weather the ongoing financial storm.

We had been realistic in our planning – we knew that life in Portugal would not be like one long holiday. We were prepared to work hard in order to live our dream, but getting this message across to friends and colleagues in the UK was impossible. Eventually, we came to accept that this was a battle we couldn't win. So, when the inevitable question came up, we simply settled for "Great, thanks" as our response.

Lisbon

Despite having lived in Portugal for over a year and a half, we had explored little of our new country beyond the Algarve coast. We had a week booked off work in September, with no firm plans other than visiting Lisbon. We had intended to have a lazy weekend and the drive up to Lisbon on either the Monday or Tuesday of our week off. However, on Friday night our plans were brought forward by the appearance of a large mouse on our balcony.

Ben is truly terrified of rodents – even photographs of them disturb him. The appearance of a mouse on our balcony escalated our vague holiday plans into a mad dash for Lisbon. While we fled there, my mother very kindly visited our apartment and removed all the plants from our balconies, including the peach tree, which was discovered to be the source of attraction for our furry little visitor.

The mouse incident and Ben's resulting reluctance to return home meant that we ended up spending five nights in Lisbon, instead of the one or two that we originally had in mind, so it did have its upside.

After a beautifully quiet cruise up the motorway to Lisbon, we reached the outskirts of the city. Lisbon is accessed from the south by the long 25 de Abril bridge, towered over by the huge and impressive Cristo-Rei statue, which overlooks the city. The two-hour traffic jam over the bridge gave us plenty of time to admire the statue, but meant that we arrived at the hotel too late to do much other than have a light supper before bed.

The next day, it was time to explore. Ben has a pretty amazing sense of direction and, having previously spent three days in Lisbon, already had a near-perfect map of the city in his head. I am the opposite – completely geographically challenged – so I let Ben do the leading. Transport passes in hand, we jumped on the metro and began the pleasurable experience of being tourists in our own country.

After an hour of wandering around and admiring the city in the sunshine, and stopping for a quick, capital-city-priced breakfast, we discovered the design museum, which was free to enter and included some fascinating exhibits. Ben was particularly taken with the iconic 1970s hi-fi systems.

Next we boarded the Elevador de Santa Justa. This is a huge and (for those with fears of heights, like me) terrifying lift that takes passengers from the lower part of the city to the Chiado and Bairro Alto districts on top of the steep hill. We paid an extra couple of euros to climb to the top of the lift's tower, so that Ben could admire the city spread out below us while I cowered in the middle trying not to look down.

The Bairro Alto, famed as Lisbon's hectic nighttime area, was strangely quiet during the day. We wandered the residential streets until we found ourselves in the pretty Praca do Principe Real park, where we stopped in the sunshine for a cool beer. While I was absorbed in our Lisbon guidebook, a man at the next table kept catching Ben's eye. The eye contact was enough for Ben to mention it to me, just at the point that I read in the book that we were sitting in a popular gay pickup spot. We finished our beers and moved on, declining the gentleman's unspoken offer!

For me, one of the main attractions about any Portuguese city is the mish-mash of old and new architecture. I love the way that crumbling, peeling old buildings are crowded in with their more glossy, modern counterparts. Lisbon is no exception. It has some stunning modern buildings, beautiful old statues and delightful crumbly houses, which make wandering round the city a real pleasure. The contrast between the wide, sun-drenched Avenida de Liberdade, with its designer shops, fountains and pavement cafes, and the cluttered, narrow streets of the Alfama district provide something for everyone and I was enchanted by it all.

We had planned to find the botanical gardens next, but after an hour of fruitless wandering we still couldn't locate them. Instead, we hopped on the metro to the large Parque Eduardo VII, stopping off at a supermarket on the way to grab provisions for a picnic. The heat-soaked park was a perfect place to sit and relax while we ate our cheese, bread, chorizo and *bolas de berlim* (very tasty and very fattening Portuguese cream doughnuts). When the persistent ants finally became more than I could bear, we headed back to the hotel for a relaxing swim.

The relaxing swim turned into a quick dip when we discovered the million or so noisy children in the hotel pool. Instead we indulged in cocktails in the hotel bar before heading out once more to the Bairro Alto. The district had transformed since our earlier stroll around it – the quiet residential streets had sprouted hundreds of lively bars and packed restaurants. Tourists and locals mixed together, enjoying the caipirinha-fuelled atmosphere.

We settled in to a restaurant for a lengthy, boozy dinner, chatting with the friendly staff about life in Portugal long after we had finished our meal. We left around midnight, intending to have a cocktail at a nearby bar and head back to the hotel. However, the Bairro Alto's electric atmosphere was too much for us to resist and instead of having one drink we had so many I lost count, visiting several bars and drinking and dancing the night away. When we finally stumbled out of a cab and into the hotel, day was dawning and guests were already in reception checking out, ready to catch early morning flights. We weaved our way to the lifts with as much dignity as we could muster.

*

Most of the following day was spent hiding in our room, watching TV and eating room-service pizza. By the afternoon we felt better and once more ventured out, this time to explore the Centro Columbo, which our guidebook informed us was the largest shopping centre in Iberia. It is located next to Benfica football stadium, so we took a couple of snapshots of the stadium before entering the shopping centre.

Once inside, we instantly regretted our choice of destination. It was packed with people and we quickly got lost among the crowds, unable to find our way to an exit. Our hangovers returned with a vengeance. Spotting a café, we sank gratefully into the chairs and ordered coffee (me) and bright green apple sorbet (Ben). We used the time to plan our next move – a military-style operation to source a DVD, some bags of popcorn and enough soft drink to fill a swimming pool. As soon as these had been obtained, we retreated back to the hotel to spend the evening watching said DVD and eating more room-service pizza.

*

By the following day our hangovers were thankfully entirely gone and we were keen to make the most of our remaining days in Lisbon (feeling immensely guilty for our laziness the day before). We got up early and took the metro to Parque das Nações. This huge area of Lisbon was developed for Expo 98 and is now a dedicated leisure/tourist zone. It provides some lovely views of the Tagus river and of the stunning Vasco de Gama bridge, which, at over 10 miles in length, is Europe's longest bridge.

We visited the water gardens (disappointingly small and poorly maintained) before joining the impressive queue for the Oceanarium. Despite Ben's grumblings about joining such a long queue, the large number of open ticket booths meant that we were quickly inside and ready to experience the marine life housed by Europe's second largest aquarium.

The Oceanarium was packed with children on school trips and getting close to the windows of the main tank was challenging at times, but we certainly saw enough to make the visit worthwhile. I was captivated by the sunfish (a rarity in aquariums) and sharks, while Ben adored the otters, which were definitely showing off for the crowds.

After a couple of hours of wandering and staring at more fish than we could count, we returned to the hotel and spent the rest of the day wallowing in the spa, which was deserted and the complete opposite of the hellish swimming pool.

*

As the next day was our last full day in Lisbon, we decided to cram in as much tourist stuff as we could manage, so set off early in the morning for Sintra, to explore the famous palace.

Our train took us through various densely housed suburbs before depositing us in the delightful hilltop town of Sintra – the complete opposite of the countless tower block filled regions through which we had just passed. Sintra is a beautiful place and has a lovely old-world feel to it. It has picturesque gardens, stunning views and a range of palaces and museums to choose from. It also hosts a number of *pastelarias* selling *queijadas* – sweet, cheese-based pastry cakes, which sound revolting but taste amazing. We bought a packet, intending to take them back to our family as a gift, but had scoffed the lot within 15 minutes.

We explored Sintra and found our way to the Palácio Nacional, where we eagerly followed the signs to the entrance. A large, firmly closed door blocked our path. We rechecked the signs and tried the door once more. It was still locked. We retreated into the sun and sat on a step to study our guidebook. It didn't take long to work out that we had visited Sintra on the only day of the week that the palace was closed.

So, after a quick photo or two of the outside of the palace, we set off to explore the rest of Sintra's offerings. Happily, this meant we had time to discover the magical toy museum, which was packed with vintage toys of all sorts. I was fascinated by the tiny Egyptian stone toys, which were over 3,000 years old. Despite the fun provided by the museum, it was rather depressing to see some of the Barbie dolls that I had played with as a child now classed as old enough to be in a museum.

With my self-image thus dented, we departed Sintra and caught the train to Cascais – the beach resort of choice for Lisboetas. It was a hot day and we were eager to cool our feet in the sea, but Lisbon's coastal offering was not quite what we had become used to in the Algarve. Cascais featured several small sandy beaches, all of which were densely covered with people competing for every square inch of sand. This was disappointing, as a relaxing stroll along the beach with our toes in the sea had been something we were particularly looking forward to. Determined not to be thwarted, we wove through the crowds, kicked off our flip-flops and plunged our feet into the sea. It was freezing – far colder than we were used to on the south coast. We lasted about five seconds before heading back through the hordes to see what the rest of Cascais had to offer.

We toured the town, pausing for a quick lunch of *bifanas* (thin pork steak sandwiches) and beers. Our wandering led us to the marina, which was preparing to host the America's Cup, but as this brought with it a large collection of ostentatiously wealthy individuals and their spoiled, noisy children, we didn't linger for long.

Instead we discovered, beneath the arch of an old stone bridge, a tiny little beach, where a small inlet reached the land between the sections of the marina. It was an oasis of calm, with just a few locals watching their children play on the sand and dipping their toes in the icy cold water. We climbed down the side of a decayed stone tower to reach it and settled into the tranquillity of the scene. It was entirely undiscovered by tourists and felt like a reward to counterbalance the crowded beaches and noisy marina that we had endured on the way. Despite the challenging water temperature, we even swam a little.

With our energy and enthusiasm restored, we strolled down to the main seafront and joined hundreds of locals and tourists in the evening promenade tradition, slowly wending our way the two or so miles along the promenade to Estoril. Having arrived in Estoril, we found it didn't have as much to offer as Cascais, so after a brief pause for ice cream in the pretty park in front of the casino as the sun began to go down, we promenaded our way straight back to Cascais for dinner, before catching a late train back to our hotel.

*

Spending time in Lisbon and discovering more of what our country had to offer was fantastic. It was particularly good to experience big-city life in Portugal. Although we adored the Algarve, with its sunshine, orange trees and beaches, there were times when we missed the variety that we used to have in London. Our break in Lisbon had given us the chance to eat food from different countries (including a particularly good Greek mezze platter), spend some time doing cultural activities and party Lisbon-style!

Ever since moving to Portugal we had toyed with the idea of moving to Lisbon, and spending a few days there had opened our eyes to the city's attractions. It had also allowed us to see the downside of such a move. Given our love of all things beach and sea-related, to move somewhere with such crowded beaches and cold water temperatures just didn't make sense. Sad though we were to leave Lisbon's attractions behind, we were also glad to return to the Algarve knowing that – for the time being at least – that was where we truly wanted to be.

Tastes of England

Around September, a stir was caused in the English expat community by the opening of a new Iceland store in the western Algarve. Although Iceland had been present in Spain for a number of years, this was its first store in Portugal.

I must confess, my first reaction was a snobby disdain for what I viewed as a budget supermarket, advertised in England by cocaine-addled celebrities feeding their families with platters of mediocre frozen party food. Then Ben enlightened me a bit – it turns out there is more to Iceland than just frozen food. Half of the store was going to be frozen and half would be groceries, including a wide range of English brands and products not previously available in Portugal.

My feelings about this were decidedly mixed. I enjoyed the Portuguese diet and certainly didn't want to be one of those expats who ate nothing but food from their country of birth. On the other hand, items like Branston Pickle and Marmite kept popping into my head. We had bought a car in Portugal, paid our tax here, completed all of our legal paperwork (despite the difficulties) and contributed every month to the economy through our rent, bills and shopping. We had worked hard to integrate into Portuguese life and respect the country and its people, so surely we shouldn't feel guilty about wanting to see which little tastes of England had now suddenly been made available to the Algarve's population?

In the end we decided to pay Iceland a visit, giving in to our English roots and seeing what they had to offer. After an hour's drive, with Ben getting more excited and saying things like, "Ooh, smoked mackerel!" every few miles, we arrived.

Any residual guilty feelings vanished the second I stepped through the door. I had no idea that there were so many English foods that I missed until they were all laid out in front of me. We spent nearly two hours trundling round the store with our trolley, having to take turns to pop out for a *bica* (a wonderfully potent Portuguese espresso) in the next-door café halfway through to give us the energy to continue.

After almost two years in Portugal, I thought that I had access to all the food that I needed on a day-to-day basis and (before going to Iceland) wouldn't have said I was lacking for anything. However, my Englishness reasserted itself with a vengeance on our way round the supermarket. I even squealed with delight when I came across the tins of golden syrup. Nor was I the only one – other English shoppers could be heard exclaiming over items ranging from tinned spaghetti hoops to Jamaican ginger cake. The Portuguese shoppers seemed to be having fun too, exploring a whole variety of items hitherto unavailable in this part of the country.

The journey home (with both the boot and back seat full of shopping) gave me time to reflect on the contrast I felt between my Englishness and my growing Portuguese-ness. I had always wanted to integrate – to learn the language, cook Portuguese food and make Portuguese friends. Ben and I had agreed that when we had children they would have Portuguese names and attend Portuguese school, rather than an English-language international school. Our intention was to be in Portugal for life, embracing its people, culture and traditions, as those were the things that had drawn us away from the UK in the first place.

When we left England, we had been deeply disillusioned

with a number of aspects of life there. We needed a change and to be part of a society which valued different things. Quality of life and family values were held in high regard in Portugal, unlike in "Broken Britain". Part of my reasons for leaving England was a rejection of a society that had developed into something I could no longer feel linked with. Perhaps this was partly why I was so determined to integrate so thoroughly into Portugal.

After living here for two years, my view had gradually changed. For all my desire to become Portuguese (which was still as strong as ever), I had come to accept that I couldn't just deny my English upbringing. It was obvious to anyone that I was not Portuguese – my skin was a lighter colour and no matter how hard I tried I always had an accent when I spoke the language.

It had gradually dawned on me that I would always, to some extent, be viewed as a foreigner. Even when I had been in Portugal long enough to be granted permanent residency and a Portuguese passport (higher powers and *câmara* permitting) I would be sure to be greeted in English when walking into strange restaurants in the summer season. I found this an irritating prospect, but knew I would have to make my peace with it.

Giving myself a hard time over my Englishness was ridiculous. I am English. No matter where I live in the world or for how long, I will always be English. That didn't mean I couldn't wholeheartedly apply myself to being Portuguese, but I had to find a happy medium by accepting my roots. As I settled down to enjoy my dinner of smoked mackerel salad, I felt more at ease with the combination of the two cultures within me than I had since I moved here.

Who would have thought that the opening of supermarket could have caused such introspection!

Career developments

Finding work in Portugal can be hard, particularly if you don't speak fluent Portuguese. Part of the reason Ben and I moved to Portugal was to get away from the London culture of working harder and harder and making more and more money until you have no time to see your children other than for two weeks of holiday each summer. We didn't want to have babies and then palm them off on a nanny. We didn't want to miss out on all those precious moments that life throws up, just because we were too busy to notice. For us, Portugal had provided an alternative way to move forward in life.

We still needed to work, of course. Life in Portugal was cheaper than in the UK, but it was certainly not free, and the global economic crisis meant that it was becoming ever more expensive. I had kept my UK job and worked hard since we had moved to Portugal to show that the arrangement could be more productive than when I was based in London. Regular trips to the UK and daily use of Skype meant that I could meet with colleagues face to face whenever I needed to. The peace afforded by my home working arrangement meant that I could turn projects and reports around far faster than I had been able to when based in the noisy office environment. The situation wasn't without its difficulties, but overall the arrangement that I had negotiated with my company was working well.

For Ben, the move to Portugal had given him the chance to

take a step back from his demanding career running his own IT business in London. He still had the business and whenever we returned to the UK would spend his days dashing from one client to the next, but in Portugal he had time to think through what he really wanted to do with his life. Initially a career break of several months had been discussed, but his active mind wouldn't allow it and instead he began to establish a writing career for himself. The work was varied, ranging from technical IT articles to website content and to lifestyle pieces for travel magazines. He enjoyed some parts of it more than others, but having the time to review how he felt about the various projects he worked on meant that he could move towards eliminating the less exciting parts and focus on the bits he really enjoyed.

After nearly two years in Portugal, Ben had established a range of income streams from clients in the UK, Europe and America. He enjoyed the variety that his writing career now afforded. He worked hard, because his perfectionist nature demanded it and because working hard came naturally to him. Work still left him short of time on occasion, but in a different way from how it had been when we had been in London. The key difference was that he now had a career which allowed him to be creative and to pick and choose the assignments he worked on. He looked forward to getting up and starting work in the morning, which had certainly not been the case for the last two years we had lived in London.

Sometimes people online would ask about moving to Portugal and finding work there. They seemed to have visions of landing in the country, speaking only English, and instantly finding work that would pay them highly enough to support their entire family. We knew from our time living here that this was utterly unrealistic. Portuguese workers are not paid well (by English standards) and work long hours. The unemployment rate is rising and young people in particular struggle to find work and establish careers. This environment is offset by a culture of living at home, usually until around the mid-thirties, in properties that have been in the family for generations and thus have no mortgages. This goes some way towards making up for the low wages, but competition for jobs is still fierce.

Depending on the time of year, the Algarve presents either considerably more or considerably fewer employment opportunities than the UK. In the summer months, tourism means that the region's population quadruples, resulting in high demand for staff in bars, restaurants and other service industries. At this time, it might indeed be possible for a non-Portuguese speaker to find work, assuming he/she was happy to work long hours for low wages. During the winter months, with most of the businesses either shut or running on a skeleton crew to serve their few customers, jobs are scarce even for the locals.

Starting your own business in Portugal was also not an easy option. Ben and I had considered doing this with a number of different ventures. Thanks to Ben's experience of setting up and running his own company in England, neither of us was averse to the idea of doing the same in Portugal – although we would be certain to choose a business that entailed regular working hours and no chance of our downtime being interrupted.

What put us off was the level of bureaucracy involved. We had already gone through such dramas with our *residência* paperwork that the idea of voluntarily becoming embroiled in the system once more seemed unthinkable. Licence applications would need to be made, along with the opening of business bank accounts, registering the company and so forth.

I consulted a friend who had married a Portuguese man and was now living with him in England. His family had opened a café to the north of Lisbon. They were Portuguese nationals and Portuguese was their native language. They had previously run a café in another area of the country. Despite all of this, it took them nearly two years to complete the paperwork and obtain the licences they needed in order to open their Lisbon venture.

Needless to say, Ben and I quickly dropped the idea of running our own business. It was a disappointing decision and I am certain that in future we will revisit the idea. We both enjoy a challenge and the idea of establishing our own company to contribute to the ailing Portuguese economy appeals for a number of reasons – some based on personal gain and others more altruistic.

For the present, we focused on our existing careers and the opportunities that these presented. We would leave the bureaucratic fight for another day – at least on the business front.

Health care

Part of our reason for agreeing to drop the idea of opening our own business in Portugal was that we were already engaged in a bureaucratic battle on another topic – health care. Once we had lived outside of the UK for more than six months and were no longer classed as residents there, our entitlement to use the National Health Service ceased. This was despite the fact that I was still paying National Insurance in the UK.

For Ben, this was not a problem – he registered as self-employed in Portugal, obtained a social security number and thus became entitled to receive a Portuguese medical card and register with a doctor.

For me, the situation was far more complicated. There are provisions within European law for those paying their social security contributions in one country to receive their health care entitlement in another country. Ben read up on this extensively for me and advised me of the document I needed to obtain from the UK in order to be eligible for health care in Portugal. I wrote to the UK authorities and thus the battle began.

To date I have filled out forms, sent letters and faxes and spent hours on the telephone explaining my situation to the UK. I have also paid a Portuguese lawyer to become involved and have visited the *Segurança Social* (social security) office in my local town on two occasions. The result of all this has been that my application for health care has repeatedly been returned to me for more information or rejected entirely by the UK authorities. Each time they wrote back to me, there was evidence that they had misunderstood my situation, despite the repeated explanations I had provided. Each time I wrote back, they kept my letter in a holding room, where it sat for two months before being opened.

After almost two years of living and working in Portugal, I had failed to convince either country that I was deserving of the right to medical care – despite paying hundreds of pounds each month to the UK in National Insurance (not to mention the NI contribution that my employer was also still making). I had taken out a private health care policy to cover any emergency situations which might arise (in either country) but pro-active things like blood pressure checks and general check-ups were denied to me. The possibility of Ben and me starting a family, without access to pre- or post-natal care, was also not an option and was something that frustrated both of us deeply.

The silliest part of the whole situation was that were I to become unemployed, I would automatically qualify for Portuguese health care as Ben's spouse. It was only because I was contributing to both the UK and Portuguese economies that I was being punished in this way – if I ceased contributing to either then suddenly I would be granted the benefit that I had been fighting for so long to obtain.

At least we had the lovely sunshine to keep our spirits high despite the irritations of the health care battle. Oh, wait, that's right . . .

Winter arrives with a vengeance

The summer ended in style in the Algarve. A wind and rainstorm blew through our sunshine paradise suddenly in the middle of one Sunday night and we were awoken by the sound of the rain battering down and the shutters rattling in the wind. The storm was so fierce that we got out of bed at 3 m and watched the lightning forking spectacularly over the ocean every few seconds.

In the morning, we awoke to a very different world than we had gone to bed in. Dashing outside to retrieve the soaking washing, which had been merrily drying in the sun the evening before, I landed ankle deep in water. Debris carried in the storm had blown onto the balcony and blocked the gutter outlets. The rain was still pouring down and, had we risen a couple of hours later, the water level would have risen sufficiently for us to have been mopping the floors inside rather than just dealing with a flooded balcony.

I cleared the gutter outlets, resulting in a torrent of water erupting from our balcony onto the street below. Luckily the driving wind and rain meant that nobody was out in the street to be soaked by the sudden waterfall.

The rain cleared by lunchtime and I ventured out in the car to buy some lunch. Debris was scattered liberally about the roads and in the street next to ours I found a palm tree with its top blown clean off by the fury of the storm. Bins had been blown over and were lying in the street and several road signs had been knocked down by the wind.

The local damage was nothing compared to that inflicted on Faro airport. Damage to the roof had resulted in a number of injuries and flights had been diverted to Lisbon and Seville. The structural damage was followed by flooding and local news stations reported that it would be months before the airport was fully repaired.

It was once more time to unload the thick jumpers, coats, scarves and gloves from the top shelves of our wardrobes. The cold weather was accompanied by coughs and sniffles for both of us, but at least it gave me the chance to refresh the "at the chemist" section of my Portuguese vocabulary. With the sunshine replaced by wind, rain and germs, we battened down the hatches, coughing and sneezing our way through our working days before collapsing in front of the television wrapped in blankets during the evenings. It was a pattern we were beginning to recognise, this being the start of our third winter in the Algarve.

One rather amusing incident alleviated our general atmosphere of feeling sorry for ourselves – the removal of the topless palm tree damaged by the storm. I spotted the workers from our back balcony, which overlooked the street concerned. They arrived in a small van with a cherry picker. By the time I saw them, the top half of the palm tree had already been disposed of, presumably by using the cherry picker. At the point I went out onto the balcony, a stump of trunk about twice the height of a man was left.

There were three workmen and no hard hats or other safety equipment anywhere in sight. As I watched, one of the workmen fired up a large chainsaw. He advanced on the tree and then held the chainsaw up over his head, as high as he could reach. He edged his way around the tree with the chainsaw held aloft, while his colleagues stood and watched, smoking.

The workman had cut almost the full way around the tree when the top half of it began to tip towards him. One of his colleagues jumped up at it and gave it a shove in the opposite direction, narrowly missing the still-running chainsaw as he did so. The top of the trunk crashed to the ground and the noise of the chainsaw stilled. All three workmen stood and smoked while looking at it.

I smiled to myself at the differences between the UK and Portugal.

The beginning

Living in Portugal had definitely turned out to be different from how we had imagined it. We had fallen in love with the country during several holidays, but living somewhere and going on holiday there are completely different experiences. Living and working in Portugal didn't provide us with that same undiluted happy holiday feeling that previous stays here had, but instead we had developed a deep-rooted happiness at being part of our new country.

When you move somewhere, real life goes with you, with all its stresses and strains. This was true for us in Portugal, but just because our new life had turned out differently than we had imagined didn't mean that it hadn't lived up to our initial hopes – quite the opposite. We had followed our hearts and didn't regret it for a moment (despite the paperwork-related challenges that life in the sun had brought with it).

Our progress in some areas had been slow, but always steady. Now when we spoke Portuguese in shops and restaurants, or chatted with our neighbours, we did it without thinking about it, rather than having to pause and translate things in our heads. We read recipes and local newspapers without trouble. Some words still bothered us and our grammar was shocking at best, but we could converse and be understood.

The wobbly days had stopped entirely. The doubts were gone – this was our life now, so what was there to be doubtful about? There had been high points and low points, but that was life.

The low points had been unexpected in some cases (that freezing cold first winter and the mouldy disaster that was our first house; the touristy craziness of July and August) and entirely expected in others (dealing with Portuguese bureaucracy). Our routine, particularly the frequent work trips to England, had taken some getting used to and was at times unsettling, but we both agreed it was better than having stayed in London.

Sadly, my dream of filling my bicycle's basket with bread and olives never quite took shape. Currently my bike is sitting in the stairwell of our apartment block, has been minus its pedals for over a year after a mishap and is still without the longed-for basket. I do intend to renovate it one day, when we have worked up the courage to tackle the full length of the Ecovia.

The high points had been amazing. Having the opportunity to share our new life with so many of our nearest and dearest had given us countless cherished memories.

The natural beauty by which we were surrounded – beaches, mountains, waterfalls, the ocean and the forest – delighted us, as it continues to do to this day.

The gastronomic wonders of this part of the world had more than lived up to our expectations – from unbelievably cheap fish feasts in local restaurants, to barbecues on the terrace, to tapas dinners just over the border in Seville.

The overall welcome we had received in Portugal was friendlier than we had ever dared to hope it would be. Various people stood out: our original neighbours in Tavira who encouraged our slow and nervous first attempts at Portuguese, the bar owner who offered us countless pieces of advice and encouragement during our wobbly moments and our new friends and neighbours in our little village. Ben had also received a great deal of advice and support from kind-hearted, helpful people he had met through the online expat forums. All of these people – and many more – made our move to Portugal so much easier than it would otherwise have been.

It had been a time of triumphs as well, albeit in some cases quite small ones – finally getting our broadband, building up our language skills, winning the battle for our *residência* and understanding when the surly girl in our local shop finally cracked a joke in Portuguese and gave us a smile.

We had learned a lot, experienced a lot and had some of the happiest times of our lives. Despite our naivety in a number of areas we had managed to overcome the obstacles that were placed in our way from time to time. Our Portuguese adventure was set to continue for years to come, with all the exciting, scary, fun, stressful and emotional moments that it was sure to bring with it.

We were living our dream.

PART 2
BEN'S PRACTICAL INFO AND TRIVIA

Now you have read Louise's account of our first two years in Portugal, perhaps your thoughts are turning to whether you could do the same? In this section, I bring you an assortment of trivia and practical information to help you to begin your own Portuguese adventure.

The A to Z of moving to Portugal

A is for Algarve

It's where we live and therefore justifiably first on this list. There is so much more to the Algarve than the well-known tourist resorts such as Albufeira – places that may well be the only areas with which tourists are familiar.

The scenery in the Algarve varies hugely, from the wild, windswept beaches of the West coast known to few foreign visitors other than surfers, via the picturesque coves of the central region, to the vast island beaches up "our end" in the East, many of which can only be reached by small ferries and fishing boats.

Many expats choose the inland Algarve, and these people usually describe their location as "up in the hills". Here, the tourist resorts feel like another world entirely, and one needn't travel too far to experience a way of life that seems unchanged for generations.

Of course, Portugal isn't only about the Algarve – in fact, residents of other areas frequently say that the Algarve isn't really like Portugal at all! While this is perhaps a little unfair, the country clearly has much more to offer – rural lifestyles in the central region, city life in Lisbon and Porto and more low-key beach life on the Silver Coast. Whatever your preferences, there is a part of Portugal to suit you – and it's worthwhile spending some time exploring before you decide where to live.

A is also for Amazon Marketplace

If you plan to have a clear-out before moving to Portugal and you have plenty of time, Amazon Marketplace is a good place to sell books and CDs in good condition, as they tend to fetch better prices than eBay. You can list as many as you have time to, then sit back and watch the moving-funds roll in.

A is also for A22

Not to be confused with the A2, which is a toll road between the Algarve and Lisbon, the A22 is a motorway that stretches almost the entire width of the Algarve, from Lagos in the West to the Spanish border at its eastern end.

The A22 was controversially turned into an electronic toll road in late 2011. The road has no tollbooths; instead, residents buy an electronic transponder that monitors their use of the road and charges the toll fees to a bank account. Tourists and visitors complain a lot about the A22 as nobody really seemed to think through how it would work for them. Residents in the Algarve also moan about tolls on the A22 – a lot.

B is for Banking

If you're going to live in Portugal, you'll need a Portuguese bank account. Getting this may be your first encounter with

Portuguese bureaucracy – so take a deep breath, set a day aside and take every piece of official documentation you can imagine. At the very least, take proof of income, proof of address, your Portuguese fiscal number and some official identification, such as a passport.

If you happen to live near London, several Portuguese banks have branches in the city, and you may be able to open an account in advance from there.

Once you have a Portuguese bank account, you may be pleasantly surprised to discover that banking in Portugal is more personal than in other countries – we know our bank manager by name and have her phone number. One reason for this is that free personal banking is less common in Portugal – instead you are often charged a small monthly fee for operating your account.

B is also for Bonkers

No matter how well you think you know your friends and family, some of them will surprise you with their attitude towards your planned emigration. Frankly, some of them will think you are bonkers.

This was an attitude that really caught us unawares when we were planning our move. For us it was logical – Portugal was preferable to England in many ways and we would have a better quality of life there. Not everyone we told saw it that way though, so be prepared that not everyone will be as pleased as you would like them to be about your forthcoming move.

C is for Cars

Cars are extremely expensive in Portugal. On the plus side, the climate in the southern half of the country means they are not prone to rust. However, anyone expecting to pick up a "good runner" for peanuts will be sorely disappointed. You'll find more about cars in the "cost of living" section.

C is also for Car boot sales

Before you move, car boot sales are tremendous fun and great for getting rid of the lower-value items that aren't worth putting up on eBay – provided you can resist the temptation to go home with more crap than you arrived with!

Nobody expects to go to a car boot sale and pay a lot for anything, so they are not the place to take high value items, though we have had some success with obscure kitchen gadgets. Also surprisingly successful are power adaptors and cables – people seemed to snap them up. Clothes seem to go well too.

Car-boot sales also give you the opportunity to meet some of the world's more unusual people. Our favourites were a strange man who perused the stalls stroking a glove puppet, and a man who claimed to be allergic to "digital waves". As a result, he was pleased to buy a tatty old analogue cordless phone from our stall. Unfortunately, he then used "interference from digital waves" as his excuse for trying to walk away from our stall without paying.

It is worth mentioning that VHS videos do not seem to be wanted by anyone (although we have since realised that there is perhaps more of a market for them here in Portugal). Your best bet for those is to drop them off in a charity shop and then leg it before they realise they are VHS videos and try to give them back!

When you have your clear-out, don't overlook friends and family when offloading your treasures. We set aside our dining room for everything we were getting rid off and insisted everyone visiting our house had a good look around our "shop". Although you end up giving a few bits away, you will find plenty of items that people are happy to pay for.

When you reach the final stages where people are collecting eBay items, buying things from you directly and handing you money at car boot sales, make sure all the money goes into the moving fund and not straight into your wallet!

A small number of car boot sales take place in Portugal, but it's fair to say they haven't truly caught on – you may just encounter other expats trying to offload the same kind of crap that you are!

C is also for Coffee

If you don't like coffee before moving to Portugal, you may well do afterwards. Coffee in Portugal is some of the best in the world and available in countless variations, from the rocket-fuel strong *bica* (an espresso), to a milky *galão* (probably the closest thing to a latte).

Those wishing to learn about the science of ordering coffee in Portugal would be well advised to check out this article: http://www.emmashouseinportugal.com/living-in-portugal/ coffee-in-portugal/

D is for Driving

Driving in Portugal is . . . different. Tailgating is something of a national pastime, as is overtaking on blind bends.

On the bright side, the volume of traffic is lower than in many other countries, at least outside of the major cities. We prefer driving in Portugal to driving in the UK for this reason, but there's no denying the importance of staying alert and defensive in your driving style.

E is for eBay

By the time we arrived in Portugal, we had sold around 800 items though our eBay account to help boost our moving fund. eBay can be wonderful and infuriating in equal measure. One of the best things about eBay is that, by using the "completed listings" feature on "advanced search", you can get a pretty good idea of what your items will sell for by taking an average from the last few times someone sold that item.

eBay is great for selling certain things: electrical and computer items, video games and musical instruments tend to consistently sell for what they are worth. Other things are less successful. Since eBay stopped allowing people to charge postage for books, there is little point in trying to sell them via eBay. If you have English language books it may, in fact, be worth shipping some – your fellow expats may be grateful for them!

We sold some furniture towards the end, and this went for upsettingly low values. Having said that, where eBay does come in handy in terms of furniture is when you stipulate in the listing that the buyer will have to dismantle the item to take it away. We managed to get rid of our king size bed, which we would never have managed to get down the stairs had the buyer not come to take it to pieces. Although it sold for less than it was worth, the fact we saved ourselves a day of work taking the thing to bits made it a fair trade.

E is also for Electrical goods

Some people will suggest you bring your electrical goods, including white goods, to Portugal with you. We disagree.

Although electrical goods can be marginally more expensive in Portugal, by law they have to have a two-year warranty, which goes some way to explaining the variation. They also have the correct plugs! By all means, bring laptops and games consoles, but think very carefully as to whether it's really worth shipping fridge freezers and washing machines – the shipping cost may mean it's cheaper to buy new ones when you arrive.

F is for Food

Portugal is a country renowned for wonderful (if often rather simple) food. Sparkling fresh fish, grilled meats and plenty of fresh fruit is the order of the day.

Outside of tourist regions and cities, it is wise to come to terms with the fact that you may not find the level of culinary variety you have been used to in your former country. If you live in the sticks, your nearest Chinese or Indian takeaway could be a long drive away.

While this can feel limiting at times, it gives you a chance to embrace the cuisine of your new home which, let's face it, is what you should be doing! Given time, Portuguese comfort food dishes such as *bacalhau a Brás* (salt cod with onions, shredded potatoes and egg) or *arroz de pato* (duck rice) may become what you crave instead.

While supermarkets abound in Portugal, you will probably find they don't offer as much variety as those in some other countries. Portuguese supermarkets are often also quite poorly stocked. Walking into an Algarve supermarket off-season with a large shopping list can lead to frustration – some things are sure to be unavailable.

Luckily, the supermarkets are complemented by local markets in most towns, which feature a wonderful selection of local produce at low prices that would provoke serious jealousy in UK foodies.

For information on the cost of some food and drink, see the "cost of living" section.

F is also for Figs

Tread carefully with these. They are available everywhere and taste delicious – but don't eat a whole packet at once as I did when I moved here. You have been warned.

F is also for Friends

Friends are really important when you move abroad – both your old friends from back home, who you will want to stay in touch and come and visit, and also the new friends you will make on arrival.

Tread slightly carefully as you begin to meet people on arrival. As with college or university, the first "friends" you meet are not necessarily the "keepers". Expat populations can be small and close-knit and this can be both good (community) and bad (gossip!)

It is wise to be realistic about the impact your move may

have on existing friendships. Make your peace with the fact that some of these may fizzle out and they may well not be those you expect. Since we have been here we have been surprised that some friendships have strengthened despite the distance and others have faded somewhat – we'd never have been able to guess which would be which.

G is for Guests

If you move to Portugal, the likelihood is that you're going to be hosting plenty of visiting guests – family members, friends and audacious people whom you didn't previously think you knew that well!

Some of these visits may provide the best times you have in Portugal – after all, who wouldn't want to show off their new home in the sunshine and their new knowledge of the local wine? Not all visits are like this; some can be a serious struggle.

Ultimately, however close you are to friends and family, spending a week or more under the same roof is quite an unusual situation. When we lived in London, friends would often crash for a night – but that was it.

When you live abroad, it's different. You'll get to know your friends and family in more "detail" very quickly. This can be wonderful – but it can also be challenging and (in just one case for us so far) friendship-ending.

It's also bloody expensive. You soon come to realise that everyone who visits you is on holiday – a holiday they have saved for – but for you, the cocktails, restaurant bills and entry fees for tourist attractions have to come out of your normal budget. If you manage to come out the other end with money for a holiday of your own, you've done very well indeed.

G is also for Get saving!

No matter how much money you think you will need to settle in to your new country, take more! There will be unexpected costs, no matter how well you research and plan. These apply to everyday life, but also to times when the aforementioned guests come to stay.

Living life like you are on holiday is tremendous fun – but if you have guests staying for 25% of the year or more, it can become expensive, so make sure you save as much as you can before you move abroad.

H is for Hire cars

Hire cars can be invaluable when you move abroad, particularly to Portugal where importing your UK car can be an expensive headache and cars are surprisingly (and terrifyingly) expensive.

Research the hire car companies available in your local area and take care to read the small print, particularly in relation to what happens if the car becomes damaged. Ensure you are fully aware of your potential liability before proceeding.

UK-based brokers that offer vehicles from a range of local hire car companies can often provide good deals. They also have the advantage that they speak English should you have any queries or problems. However, dealing directly with a local company can also have its advantages – particularly if you are looking to negotiate a rate for a long-term hire, where local managers have more flexibility and discretion than brokers do. Long-term hire can be a viable option in the winter period, and was a great help to us while we were looking for a car of our own.

Whichever option you choose, ensure that you are confident

that you are using a reliable company and know what to do in the event of any problems.

H is also for Holidays

As I say repeatedly on my blog, living in Portugal is nothing like being on holiday here. Don't be surprised when you sometimes feel like you need to get away from Portugal after putting your heart and soul into moving there!

H is also for Health care

Don't assume that you instantly qualify for state health care when you get to Portugal. Unless you are of retirement age, this is unlikely to be the case. If you are of retirement age, and coming from the UK, the UK should give you a form, known as an S1, which will allow you to register in Portugal.

A lot of nonsense is talked about health care entitlement, so be wary of some of the misinformation on web forums, much of which is based on knowledge of the system before it was tightened up.

Basically, you are unlikely to be able to register at a state doctor's surgery until you have a social security number. You won't get a social security number unless you get a job or register as self-employed. Plenty of people will tell you different. Indeed, plenty of people managed to register with no problems a few years ago, but some of these people are now being greeted with "computer says no" when they visit the doctor and can't supply a social security number.

Research your individual situation thoroughly, and be aware that you may need to pay for a private policy to bridge the gap.

Many people in Portugal, expats and locals alike, pay to see the doctor through choice, at one of the many private medical centres throughout the country. This reduces waiting time.

I is for Internet

The Internet is your friend in Portugal – for translations, maps, restaurant reviews, expat forums, and, of course, your favourite expat blogs!

It is well worth setting up a "Portugal" folder within your browser bookmarks to keep a record of all the useful information you find.

If you are a tech-savvy type, an Internet-enabled smartphone can also be invaluable on the move, especially if you need to translate something quickly to avoid looking daft!

I is also for Islands

It comes as a surprise to some first-time visitors to the East Algarve that many of our beaches are, in fact, on sand-spit islands and only reachable by boat. The beautiful, unspoiled islands of Culatra, Armona and the Ilha de Tavira are essential places to visit.

A little further afield, Portugal boasts the Azores archipelago and the islands of Madeira and Porto Santo. As well as being wonderful holiday destinations, these may be places to consider moving to. These islands export wonderful food products to mainland Portugal. Be sure to try Azores butter and cheese (look for "Ilha" on the label), and sweet pineapples and cucumbers from Madeira.

J is for Jobs

Jobs are practically non-existent in Portugal – this is a fact, and not just something us expats say repeatedly on forums to discourage people from coming and crowding our beaches. See the "finding work in Portugal" section for more information.

K is for Kids

Giving your children the opportunity to grow up experiencing another country's culture can be an amazing experience for them. They will learn and discover things that they never would have in England, and will grow up with a much less narrow view of the world in which we live.

However, moving abroad with children can also have its pitfalls – they may not settle in or make friends easily, which can crush confidence at a key stage of development. Sending them to a Portuguese-language school will be hard for them if they don't speak the language fluently and could affect their educational achievements. Most would agree that if it is your intention to send your children to local school, it is better to do it at as young an age as possible.

As an alternative, putting children into a costly international school may improve their grades, but may isolate them from their Portuguese peers.

Nothing about moving abroad with kids is insurmountable and doing so can bring unexpected benefits, but make sure you plan carefully and keep a close eye on your children after the move to ensure they are as happy in their new country as you are.

I highly recommend the "Hands in Portugal" blog for

anyone considering moving here with children:
http://handsinportugal.wordpress.com/

K is also for Kappa

The letter "K" doesn't really exist in the Portuguese language and is only used for imported words. It is said as "kappa" when reciting the Portuguese alphabet. "W" and "Y" aren't part of the standard Portuguese alphabet either. This leads us nicely on to . . .

L is for Language

Portuguese is not an easy language to learn but, like anything, with time and effort dedicated to it, it can be done. Immersing yourself in the language as early as you can will bring rewards when you finally make the move.

There is a wide range of language learning resources available for European Portuguese, including books, CDs, free downloadable software, evening classes, private lessons, etc. Whatever your preferred learning style and weekly schedule, try and fit in at least a couple of hours of practice each week. It will make life seem so much less intimidating when you arrive in your new country.

Practice is essential, so speak and listen to others speaking Portuguese as often as you can. Listen to Portuguese radio stations or find other sources of the language to get your ears tuned to its sound. Spoken Portuguese and written Portuguese are very different, so make sure you practise speaking as well as reading and writing the language.

Early attempts at making yourself understood in Portugal can be intimidating, but the Portuguese appreciate the effort

– and will gently help you and correct you if you run into difficulties. The fact that you are trying to speak the language will set you apart from the tourists and be very much appreciated. You will find recommended books and Internet resources in the Web directory and recommended reading sections.

M is for Markets

There is no shortage of markets in Portugal. They range from daily produce and fish markets in local villages with just two or three stalls, via huge food markets in larger towns, up to monthly regional markets selling everything from live ducks and chickens to Ralph Lauren knock-offs.

Don't ignore these markets – make use of them! You'll find items you can't get anywhere else. For example, in the Algarve it can be very hard to find spring onions – but at Moncarapacho's monthly market, they are everywhere! Markets are also the place where you find the real beating heart of the country.

Think about what you're buying though – you'll find just as much tat as you will anywhere else in the world!

M is also for Money management

Money management is no easier in Portugal than it is anywhere else. While many day-to-day pleasures, such as delicious coffees and cakes, remove coins from one's purse instead of notes, there are just as many opportunities to overspend.

Remembering this is particularly important if you are moving to Portugal to downsize, with a corresponding drop in income. We found it took some time to condition ourselves away from our London spending habits – and ended up with credit card bills to prove it.

N is for Neighbours

We never had much of a relationship with our neighbours in the UK. It didn't help that one of them was an unfriendly old lady with an obsession with tree surgery (on *our* trees), but still.

Neighbours are far more neighbourly in Portugal. This may first manifest itself as semi-intrusive staring, but stick with it and you will find that your neighbours can become allies, friends and the first people to help you with your stuttering attempts at Portuguese.

O is for Officials

Respect for authority (and one's elders) is a key part of Portuguese culture. Officials expect this, so it is important to be polite and deferential to everyone from police officers to council officials to train guards. If not, your life will become difficult.

Portugal is not like the UK, where back-chatting officials is an everyday thing. While this may take some adjustment, it makes the country a far better place to be. "Remember when kids respected their elders?" They still do here.

O is also for Oranges

It's quite amusing when guests get so excited about the orange trees all over Portugal. We did as well at first, and they do look (and smell) wonderful.

The oranges themselves, however, are everywhere in the Algarve, to the point you can't get rid of them! Everyone seems to have a family with some land and some oranges, and there's only so much juice, sorbet and orange cake anyone can get through. This is why our family is determined to turn them into booze. This ambition has had varied success so far.

P is for Public transport

Using public transport is a cheap and reliable way to navigate around Portugal. Just like London, Lisbon is a place where car-free life is possible and arguably easier. Daily travel cards for the Lisbon area only work out at around €4 a day – a pleasant surprise to someone used to paying well over £10 in London.

Of course, public transport is only of use in areas it covers. Even here in the Algarve, there are places with only a very infrequent bus service. Some bus routes don't run at all at the weekend. The Algarve's single train route is better, but very slow from end to end, taking at least double the time of a road journey. In addition, many of the Algarve's stations are nowhere near the towns they serve, landing foot passengers with a bus or cab journey at the end.

So, while Portugal has good and affordable public transport, a car is still a necessary evil in many areas.

P is also for Packing

However many boxes and rolls of bubble wrap you buy, you will end up needing more. Buying these things from a storage company can cost a small fortune, so plan ahead and buy them in bulk from eBay. You'll save money and the postman will bring them directly to your door, meaning all your time and energy can be spent on packing.

Do not underestimate how long the packing will take and how much work is involved! The best plan is to lure friends and family round with the promise of beer, pizza and recreational drugs, then force them to help you pack – it really will make a difference (and they will forgive you when they get to come and stay with you for free in your new country).

P is also for Passports

First off, if you only have a short term to run on your passport, get it renewed before you move. You'll find it much easier to do it from home than you will from Portugal.

Secondly, it is actually a legal requirement to carry identification with you at all times in Portugal. While Portuguese citizens have an ID card, for foreign residents, this ID should really be your passport. Many expats, us included, balance the risk of losing it with the chance of being asked to show it, and instead carry a photocopy in their wallet. If you are the kind of person who mislays things, then this may be a good option for you.

P is also for Phones

Portugal has a good, mature telecoms infrastructure. We have found mobile phone signals to be more consistent than in the UK, even in rural areas. Calls, however, can be pretty expensive, especially if you call "home" a lot. Time after time, we kick ourselves for lazily using our landline to call friends and family rather than using our cheap and dependable Skype accounts.

Q is for Quality of life

A large and common motivation for moving abroad is improved quality of life. While it is admirable to pursue this goal, don't forget that you will be taking the daily chores of life with you to your new country. Grocery shopping, washing up and ironing do not all go away just because you live abroad. Don't assume that all chores will vanish and you will automatically have hours more free time than you used to. Wherever you move to, life goes with you!

Neither should you assume that you will suddenly turn into a different person when you arrive in Portugal. If you're an unmotivated couch potato, you won't suddenly become a gym bunny because the sun shines more regularly.

That said, it is certainly possible to improve your quality of life by moving abroad – just be realistic.

R is for Renting (property)

Renting your first property in Portugal makes a lot of sense. In fact, we strongly believe that everyone should do it. However well you have researched a move, you may get here and absolutely hate it! Maybe it will be too hot or too quiet in winter – or perhaps you will choose an area that doesn't suit your lifestyle.

Long-term rental in Portugal is inexpensive, straightforward and easy to find – take advantage of it.

R is also for Residency

Yes, Portugal is part of the EU. Yes, EU citizens have freedom of movement. *But* EU citizens must still register their residence in the country if they wish to stay for more than three months. Plenty of non-legit expats will tell you differently but this is a fact.

Part 1 of this book goes into great detail about the fun and games we had in getting our residency. It's enough to put anyone off, but it is a must for anyone who wishes to do things properly. We had a harder residency journey that most, so don't be unduly perturbed.

Immigrants from elsewhere in the world have their own residency rules. The best first port of call is the SEF (*Serviço de Estrangeiros e Fronteiras*).

R is also for Rain

The holiday brochures don't show pictures of Portugal on black, rainy days. When it rains here it *rains*. We are not talking about grey, London-style drizzle – we are talking about heavens opening, apocalyptic, very wet rain. In the winter of 2009 it did this for weeks on end. Bring an umbrella and a couple of board games.

On the bright side, the southern half of the country has an average rainfall of zero millimetres in July and August – so you can be fairly certain that your summer barbecue and beach plans won't be written off at the last minute, as they can so frequently be in Northern Europe.

S is for Sunshine

Better weather plays a large part in many people's reasons for moving abroad. It certainly did in our decision to move to Portugal. Make sure you take plenty of sun cream and sun-hats with you – you will undoubtedly need more than you imagine. It's also wise to check the costs of products like sun cream in the country to which you are moving. In Portugal, we have to pay around €15–20 for sun-cream, whereas in the UK we used to take advantage of two-for-one offers in high street chemists. Given the amount of sun-cream needed in the height of Portuguese summer, this can become an expensive habit.

Make sure your guests are prepared for the sun as well, particularly if they haven't visited Portugal before and don't realise how quickly it is possible for skin to burn in mid-summer. Our relative's intensely painful, lobster-red feet should be a lesson to anyone reading this!

S is also for Shoestring (budget)

We often see threads on expat forums from people planning to move to Portugal on a shoestring budget. While we admire anyone wishing to give it a go, sometimes you can see a mile off when certain plans are going to end in tears.

All I really need to say is that it is just as possible to be skint and miserable in Portugal as it is anywhere else.

S is also for Social security

Portugal's social security (*segurança social*) system provides for unemployment benefit, health care, state pensions and various other benefits.

With a few exceptions, it really only gives out if you put in, so anyone working here should expect to be paying it. For self-employed people, the minimum contribution, in the region of €180 per month at the time of writing, is a lot higher than it is in other European countries (though not as high as it is in Spain).

If you wish to get state health care, draw a pension and become a fully paid-up member of Portuguese society, social security will factor into your life somewhere, so get advice from an accountant to find out how it affects you.

T is for Taxation

Sadly, they have tax in Portugal too, so one of the first things any new immigrant needs to do is find an accountant – there's one recommended in the web directory section.

Income tax is pretty high in Portugal. While the ability for married couples to combine their allowances and various tax-deductible items makes some people better off here than in their former countries, couples like us who both work and earn a semi-decent level of income may find their tax liability higher than it was "back home".

U is for Unemployment

Unemployment, especially amongst the under-25s, is very high in Portugal. I've already said earlier in this A to Z how hard it is to get a job– but it's so important I'm mentioning it again.

V is for Value for money

Many items in Portugal offer great value for money: delicious wine, fresh fish and restaurant meals being just three.

Don't be fooled, however, into thinking that Portugal is a place where "buyer beware" is any less important. We often visit our local market and don't see any fish we would be happy to buy, or abandon plans for a specific Sunday lunch because all the chicken looks ropey.

Shop around, learn from your mistakes and be adventurous but cautious. As a new arrival, you're going to get ripped off a few times.

W is for Working

If part of your life in Portugal is going to involve working, you need to know that motivation can be difficult. This is especially true in the Algarve in July and August when it's very, very hot and everyone around you is on holiday.

If you are going to be working from home, make sure that you have the right mindset, especially if you haven't done it before. Buckling down to business when all you can hear is people outside splashing into a pool is tortuous and takes great willpower!

W is also for Waiting

You'll be doing quite a lot of waiting in Portugal; waiting for government departments to respond, waiting for services to be connected and waiting for the people in front of you in queues to finish their conversations.

Make your peace with it. You're in southern Europe now. Wine helps.

X is for Xenophobia

Sadly, there's no getting away from it; xenophobia exists and you will encounter it occasionally, both from the (very infrequent) person here who gives you attitude because you aren't Portuguese and from the people back home who will vent offensive, ill-informed views about your new country.

Ignore these people, ignore the *Daily Mail* and rise above it. The vast majority of people in the world are friendly, welcoming and inclusive.

Y is for Yearning (for "home")

At some point, no matter where you move to, you will experience yearnings for things from "home". This is a natural part of moving abroad, as you will be leaving behind most of that which you have taken for granted for the majority of your life.

Make sure that friends and family bring you a few treats each time they come to visit. That small pot of Marmite they squeeze into their suitcase can be invaluable when you are experiencing yearnings for the foodstuffs of your former country.

Less definite yearnings can be harder to deal with. Feelings of homesickness can be intense and strike without warning. These will lessen the longer you live abroad and are part of the process of emigrating, so try to accept them for what they are and know that they will pass soon. (If they don't, maybe it's time to re-examine how happy you are in your new country.)

After a while, it's likely that these yearnings for your former country will disappear completely. For us, trips to the UK now make us yearn to be back in Portugal, as we miss our new home.

Z is for Zeal

Above all, make sure you approach your new country with zeal, getting the most out of every experience. There will be high points and low points, but it will all be part of the wonderful adventure of moving abroad. Good luck.

The cost of living in Portugal

This section is an expansion on a very popular post that I produced for the blog. It goes into a little more detail and includes some additional information on the cost of communications.

Cost of living is about far more than the simple cost of individual items and services. One mistake many new immigrants make is to focus too much on comparing like for like. If you plan to move to Portugal only to eat English food, drink English drink and watch English TV, then things will get far more expensive than they need to.

Living like the locals enriches the experience of moving abroad, so you will notice that I have added some tips on where savings can be made.

Accommodation costs in Portugal

An excess of empty property has pushed down accommodation costs in Portugal. I won't try to provide sample costs of property for purchase, as prices vary from area to area, and estate agents' websites will give you a far better idea than I ever could.

Despite some bargain prices, unless you have a hefty

deposit the economic climate may preclude you from getting a mortgage. This isn't necessarily a bad thing right now. Continuing instability in the Eurozone and the chance that prices may get lower still means that renting for a while can be a good plan. For new expats, this should always be the strategy anyway – why not give yourself a chance to check that Portugal is definitely right for you before committing, and get a feel for the exact area you wish to live in?

The excess of empty property in Portugal is pushing down rents a little. In the East Algarve, a good two-bedroom apartment with shared pool can be found for around 400 euros a month. In more rural and less touristy parts, you will find options for less than this, while more urban areas will be more expensive.

1000 euros a month puts you into "villa with a private pool" territory. Given that you can pay more than this for a poky flat in a nasty area of London, this is one of the areas where Portugal can still be considered cheap.

TIP: You *really* need to be in Portugal to find the full selection of available rental options. In our area, almost everyone you meet knows someone who is renting apartments, and few of these ever find their way onto English language websites.

Utility costs in Portugal

Obviously, I can only guide you based on our experiences – everyone's utility usage differs. Our costs are based on two people, year round, in an apartment with two bedrooms and two bathrooms. We work from home so are in all day, and we don't hold back in terms of using air-conditioning or heating. We run various computers, a fridge freezer, cooker, washing machine and dishwasher. Our gas is purely for water heating and the hob. For around eight weeks of the year, there are four or more people here as we have guests staying.

Our costs currently average out at:

Electricity	€80 a month (includes TV licence)
Gas	€35 a month
Water	€35 a month

Taxation in Portugal

It's impossible to go into much detail on taxation, as everyone's situation is different, but taxes have increased in recent years as part of Portugal's austerity measures. In our own experience, with earnings that are mid-range for the UK but very high for Portugal, we pay significantly more income tax than we would in the UK. Across our entire income, we pay around 36%.

Some professions can take advantage of the non-habitual resident scheme and pay a flat rate of 20%. Married couples with only one worker can combine their allowances and perhaps end up better off than in their former country.

Everyone needs good accountancy advice. It took us a long time to find an accountant we could rely on – you will find details in the web directory section.

Social security should be mentioned here too. If you are self-employed and working on green receipts (*reciebos verdes*), the minimum monthly social security payment in most circumstances is around 185 euros. The size of this bill shocks some people – it doesn't, however, kick in until you have been self-employed here for around 13 months.

Motoring costs in Portugal

It shocks our friends when we tell them that petrol in Portugal is as expensive as in the UK, if not more so.

Driving in general is expensive here. Road tolls are widespread and the free roads that can be used as an alternative are no fun at all. To give you an idea of toll costs, a one-way journey from the Algarve to Lisbon costs around €19 in tolls, and a trip from one end of the Algarve to the other on the A22 is around €10.

All this, of course, is if you have a car, and there comes the biggest shock of all: cars are terrifyingly expensive, and this is particularly relevant at the lower end of the market. The kind of cars that go for £500 in the back of the UK's *Autotrader* will set you back up to €4000 here. This is offset a little by the fact that the climate means cars don't really rust, but the "cheap little runner" doesn't exist here.

Even when talking about nearly new, costs differ massively from those in northern Europe. Our car cost around €11,500 euros and we could probably have found the same for around £7000 in the UK – the exchange rate does *not* cancel that out!

Car tax is dependent on emissions – we only pay about €80 a year. However, relatives with a gas guzzling sports car almost have to place an extra zero on the end of that figure!

Communications costs

Most modern families want a full TV, Internet and phone package. The most common local packages are those from Meo (part of Portugal Telecom) and Zon. Both have a similar assortment of channels (the vast majority of which contain American content such as CSI, Family Guy and The Simpsons).

A full package, including unlimited Internet, lots of channels and a landline runs to about €60 per month. Phone calls, other than local calls to landlines, which expats won't use much, can push the bill up significantly. With the occasional call to the UK when we are too lazy to use Skype, it is not unheard of for our bill to be over €100 a month.

The cellular network is well developed in Portugal – many large towns and cities have 4G Internet and the service is more reliable than we experienced in the UK. Prices are similar, perhaps slightly higher. The key difference is that there is less of an incentive to take out a contract deal with a mobile provider. Phones are not as heavily subsided, so most people buy a phone and go on Pay As You Go. We spend between €20 and €40 a month each, which includes the occasional UK call and plenty of mobile Internet.

Food and drink costs

It's still possible to live cheaply here *if* you are prepared to eat Portuguese style. This means concentrating on pork and chicken, basic fresh salad ingredients and vegetables, in-season fish and lots of beans and rice.

Once you get into imported items, things get more expensive, though perhaps not as much so as a couple of years ago.

Supermarkets seem to be wising up to the items that expats want and things like curry pastes, Mexican ingredients and Heinz baked beans have got a little (if not much) cheaper. Of course, British expats in the Algarve also now have Iceland in Albufeira!

The longer you live in Portugal, the more you learn to spend less on food and drink. First off, many people here have families with land. Once you get to know people, you may find you have more free oranges, apricots and figs than you know what to do with!

You also get a feel for what to buy where. It's possible for us to spend either €1 or €4 on the same jar of pesto within five miles of our front door, depending on the supermarket we choose.

It's all about visiting the markets and getting friendly with stallholders, finding out who to go to for clams and when the ladies come round with the huge, cheap boxes of strawberries. Portugal is a perfect place for those who can visualise that huge box of strawberries as a cake, a sorbet and a few jars of jam.

However, those who want convenience food and UK-style supermarket shopping are likely to pay heavily for the privilege and miss out on what Portugal really has to offer.

On to drink; yes, wine is still cheap (we are currently working our way through a very drinkable red Capataz that came in a 5 litre box for just €5!) Beer is cheap too, if you stick to local brews, but if you start picking up Corona and Carlsberg, it can be more expensive than in the UK. If you're struggling to find the good cheap wines, I recommend looking at the Food and Wine Portugal blog's wine section!

A final tip: much of Portugal is very close to Spain. It's worth getting used to the things that are cheaper or better there. We go every couple of months and come back with Mexican ingredients, Iberico ham, asparagus and good cider. International shopping can be fun.

Entertainment costs in Portugal

If entertainment means eating out, then Portugal can be a bargain, with many places offering bargain three-course meals and *pratos do dia*.

Of course, in the cities and the touristy parts of the Algarve, the sky's the limit. We have Michelin-starred restaurants and beachfront bars that aren't scared to charge €8 for a *mojito*, but it's possible to have cheaper fun almost everywhere, if, of course, you have the self-discipline to stick to the cheaper restaurants and bars.

For expats, entertainment often means spending time with friends from back home, either in Portugal or in another country. Here things get expensive.

Flight costs are on the up. When we first moved to Portugal in 2009, it wasn't unusual for my wife and me to manage to both get to London and back for under £100 off-season. Bargains like this just don't seem to exist any more. Baggage charges and other fees have started to get daft too.

Even worse can be trips back for work or weddings, when travel dates are non-negotiable – £400 each to London and back is not unheard of.

When friends and family come to Portugal, things get expensive too. Essentially, you have to get used to continuously being with people who are on holiday. Wonderful though this is, people on holiday want to go to beachfront bars, eat in good restaurants and drive to see the sights.

Although people invariably pay their way, it's impossible to avoid the fact that being on holiday is expensive, even if you live in the country. All expats should be aware of this.

I'm going to finish off with the costs of a selection of random items:

	€
1 bottle of Super Bock in a supermarket	0.60
1 bottle of Corona in a supermarket	1.30
Pack of 6 thin (*bifana*) pork steaks	1.50
2 x fillet steaks from an English butcher	15.00
1 bottle of mouthwash	6.00
Paracetomol (16 pack)	2.50
Cough syrup	15.00
6 fresh sardines from market	2.00
Bottle of drinkable red wine (Real Lavrador)	1.50
Bottle of rather good red wine (Monte Velho)	3.80

Finding work in Portugal

The "Finding Work in Portugal" article, reproduced here, was very popular on the Moving to Portugal blog. Many expats commented that it had a very accurate view of how hard it is to find employment in Portugal. However, it also suggests some ways to take work with you. I have updated this text slightly to reflect some of the changes since the global financial crisis, which, sadly, have made the chances of finding work here even smaller than before.

The sure-fire way to get short shrift as a new member of any of the expat forums is to make your first post read something like this:

> "Hi, I've been to Albufaira couple of times and think I want to move to Portugal. Can ne1 tell me how to find work in Portugal. I am a secretary and my hubbie is a plasterer. We dnt speak any Portugese but are happy to lern."

Posts like this appear a lot, and their authors tend to get somewhat savaged by the old hands! The fact is, the employment situation is the main reason why expats who fancy a life in the sunshine can't just pack their things and get on the next Easyjet flight.

Getting work in Portugal

If you only spoke Portuguese, Russian or Mandarin, would you expect to be able to arrive in England or the USA and quickly find a job in your chosen field? Of course not! So let's start off there.

If you cannot speak Portuguese, your employment prospects are not exactly zero, but they *are* crap. Let's be honest about that. Although I'm not looking for a job, I have done a lot of research in terms of the kind of jobs I *could* do and I know plenty of people locally. All I have really seen in the Algarve is very low-paid seasonal bar and restaurant work and jobs selling property, which are invariably commission only.

If you happen to be 18 years old, with a free room in your parents' villa, fancying a summer of sand, sangria and Sagres, you might find what you are looking for. Fancy a permanent move? Not so much.

When I say "very low-paid," I do *mean* very, especially by British or American standards. Legal minimum wage here is around 450 euros per month *before* tax and social security, and a lot of workers are on this wage. Note that I said "legal" minimum wage. If you don't speak Portuguese and are after casual catering work, being offered €12 plus tips for a six- or seven-hour cash-in-hand shift is quite possible – I've spoken to youngsters getting this much.

If you can speak good Portuguese, obviously you have a few more options and the combination of fluency in Portuguese and English can be quite desirable. However, high unemployment after the financial crisis means that there is plenty of competition for each job. The wages are still scarily low compared to "back home" too. The average annual Portuguese wage is around €8500. Obviously some people do earn a lot more than this, but it depends on the field you are in. You should also consider the fact that most highly paid jobs are not down in the sunny Algarve, but more likely in the main cities of Lisbon and Porto.

Starting your own business

Before I descend too far into doom and gloom, all is not necessarily lost. If you are of an entrepreneurial persuasion there's no real reason why a good business idea cannot succeed in Portugal, although the language barrier could affect both the ease of setting it up and your ability to attract local customers as well as fellow expats. The tax and social security implications are also very important here – professional advice is essential.

Before going too far down the road of setting up on your own, it is essential that you know Portugal and understand its culture. Never assume that something that would work in your home country will work in Portugal – cultural differences can mean that something that would be a huge success back home may be met with indifference or lack of understanding here.

Starting a business is an option, however, and you are likely to find some of the start-up costs lower than back home, especially as buildings and offices are cheap and easy to find.

Be sure to remember that in the case of any service business, you will be competing with local companies and therefore have to pitch your pricing realistically. Also, some trade qualifications won't be valid here, so don't assume you can come here and be an electrician or plumber, without retaking your exams – in Portuguese.

Working remotely from abroad

Depending on what you do for a living, your existing employer may be persuaded to let you become a remote worker. You will need a progressive, modern-thinking boss for this to be an option, but there are benefits to your company as well as to you. Remote access technologies, Skype and cheap broadband mean that other than providing your physical presence, there is little you can't do sitting in your living room in Portugal that you can do in the office.

Try to sell your boss on a higher level of productivity, fewer interruptions, higher morale, more time for actual work, less time commuting and a reduction in office costs. If you currently work in the UK there isn't even a time difference to worry about.

Old-school bosses, jealous fellow employees and having a job that requires your physical presence, can all serve to prevent this from being an option, but it's worth considering. The Internet has made a "global workforce" a reality, and if you are a valued employee working for a forward thinking employer, they may be more open to suggestions than you would expect.

Working online

Whatever you do, don't just open Google and type "make money online". At least 99% of the things that come up will be scams. There are, however, some online work options that are a reality, as long as you accept that nothing is instant and all require you to put in hard graft.

If you can write and have experience you can sign up to online content providers such as Brighthub, Demand Media or Media Piston.

Online work providers such as Elance and ODesk are possibilities too. These marketplaces allow you to bid for contracts to provide a huge range of services: secretarial work, virtual assistance, proof reading, customer service – the list is endless.

Sounds good, doesn't it? If you have the relevant skills, it can be – but there is a "but", as there always is. You are competing for these jobs with providers in India and the Philippines who are bidding to work for $2 an hour. There are however, people out there happy to pay fairly for your skills; you just have to put a lot of time into finding them, and accept you may have to do some low-paid tasks to build up the strong feedback required to allow you to get a look in with the decent employers.

If you can do IT work and/or web design, you should be able to find work to do remotely, especially if you already have clients from back home. IT brings me tidily onto IT skills in general, which are essential for any online working opportunity – if you can't get quickly and proficiently around a computer, online working is probably not for you!

How realistic it is to earn a living from Portugal really depends on your skills and how far you are willing to take a risk. Working for yourself brings with it no sick pay, holiday pay, pension, free training or any of the other trappings of working for an employer, so it's not for everyone. Similarly, working remotely can bring with it a feeling of isolation and being out of the loop.

Nothing's perfect or simple, but one or a combination of these options may bring you sufficient income to live in the sun. We left behind a lot of security and ready cash in order to live in Portugal – and no amount of money would drag us back.

The Portugal web directory

The following is a list of all the websites that have been useful to us before, during and since our move to Portugal. You will find official sites with information on things like tax and *residência* and links to forums, blogs and articles that have helped and/or entertained us.

You will find an up to date version of this list on the Moving to Portugal blog at

http://www.movingtoportugal.org/portugal-web-directory/

and if you visit this page, you can save yourself from having to type the links, and simply click on them instead!

English-language papers

As well as local news, these papers are a valuable source of classified ads where you could find cars, property (including long term rentals) and, if you are very lucky, jobs!

THE PORTUGAL NEWS:
http://www.theportugalnews.com/

THE ALGARVE RESIDENT:
http://www.algarveresident.com/main.asp

GET REAL WEEKLY:
http://www.getrealweekly.com/

Portuguese banks

It is worth noting that several of the Portuguese banks have branches in London so people moving from the UK may be able to arrange their bank account before their arrival.

BANCO ESPIRITO SANTO:
http://www.bes.pt/

CAIXA GERAL DE DEPOSITOS:
http://www.cgd.pt/Pages/default.aspx

MILLENNIUM:
http://www.millenniumbcp.pt/

BARCLAYS PORTUGAL:
http://www.barclays.pt/

SANTANDER TOTTA PORTUGAL:
http://www.santandertotta.pt/

Property purchase

GUIDE TO PROPERTY PURCHASE:
Information on the process
http://www.portugal-info.net/info/buyingselling.htm

PURE PORTUGAL:
Primarily property in central Portugal; also offers rentals
http://www.pureportugal.co.uk/

GEKKO PORTUGAL:
Property listings and a lot of information about living in Portugal
http://www.gekkoportugal.com/

CASA SAPO:
Huge classifieds site
http://casa.sapo.pt/

Property rental

EAST ALGARVE PROPERTY RENTAL:
Letting agency based in Tavira, one of few agencies with an online list of long term rentals
http://www.east-algarve-property-rentals.com/eng-long-term-rentals.htm

RENTAL PROPERTY ON EXPATS PORTUGAL:
Mostly in Central Portugal.
http://rentals.expatsportugal.com/

(Also see classified ads in the English-language papers listed above, all available online; and the Sapo classified site, also listed above.)

Cars

MATRICULATION:
Good forum thread on successful matriculation of a UK car:
http://britishexpats.com/forum/showthread.php?t=659653&page=2

SAPO:
Huge classifieds site, many second hand cars searchable by area
http://auto.sapo.pt/carros/

DRIVING LICENCES:
Important forum thread about driving on a UK licence:
http://www.expatsportugal.com/phpBB2/viewtopic.php?t=9399

(Also see classified ads in the English-language papers listed above, all available online.)

Car hire

ECONOMY CAR HIRE:
We use this provider more than once a month – prices are good and cars are fully insured
http://www.economycarhire.com/click.php?adm=389&adt=14

Tax and finance

FINANCAS:
English language area of Financas site including guide to Portuguese tax system
http://info.portaldasfinancas.gov.pt/NR/rdonlyres/F2D76036-A62A-4BEF-9AA3-6A7B34F53371/0/Portuguese_Tax_System_CEF.pdf

ALGARVE TAX SOLUTIONS:
Our accountants – highly recommended
http://algarve-taxsolutions.com/

BLEVIN FRANKS:
High end company offering international tax advice
http://www.blevinsfranks.com/

HMRC:
Moving Abroad section of UK HMRC
http://www.hmrc.gov.uk/incometax/tax-leave-uk.htm

THIS IS MONEY:
A detailed article about pensions, tax and savings when moving abroad
http://www.thisismoney.co.uk/mortgages-and-homes/homes-abroad/article.html?in_article_id=423182&in_page_id=505

Health care

AFPOP:
The Association for Foreign Residents and Property Owners in Portugal has special rates with a number of health insurance providers
http://www.afpop.com/

PPP AXA:
Several Europe and worldwide health insurance policies offered
http://www.axappphealth care.co.uk/international-health-insurance

NHS LIVING ABROAD:
A very useful guide to what you are entitled to in terms of medical care when you move to Portugal from the UK
http://www.nhs.uk/chq/Pages/1963.aspx?CategoryID=68&SubCategoryID=159

NHS FORM CA8454:
An essential form to fill in for those resident in Portugal but still working in the UK
http://www.hmrc.gov.uk/forms/ca8454.pdf

Residência

YOUR EU:
Interesting site with details of right of residency etc.
http://ec.europa.eu/youreurope/nav/en/citizens/services/eu-guide/living/index_en.html

SEF:
English language section of SEF website
http://www.sef.pt/portal/V10/EN/aspx/page.aspx

TAVIRA IMMIGRANT PORTAL:
An attempt by Tavira Camara to put all info in one place
http://imigrante.cm-tavira.pt/index.php?mlingua=en

Forums

Such a useful source of information!

EXPATS PORTUGAL:
www.expatsportugal.com

BRITISH EXPATS:
http://britishexpats.com/forum/forumdisplay.php?f=89

EXPAT FORUM.COM:
http://www.expatforum.com/expats/portugal-expat-forum-expats-living-portugal/

Recommended reading

There is plenty of reading material available about Portugal. The very best is listed here. To make life easy, I suggest visiting this list online via the Moving to Portugal blog, where you will find links to all the books:

http://www.movingtoportugal.org/2012/07/books-about-portugal-and-an-announcement/

Moving abroad / Moving to Portugal

Buying Property in Portugal by Gabrielle Collison (ISBN 978 1907498565) is the first book I recommend to people planning a move, and not just because it includes a case study on my wife and me! The book was updated in 2011 and contains a ton of useful and (importantly) current information.

Live and Work in Portugal by Guy Hobbs (ISBN: 978 1854583338) is another tome we referred to before we moved. Sadly, it hasn't been updated in several years and, let's face it, the world was a very different place economically in 2005. Still, it's cheap and worth a read!

Au Revoir Angleterre: Making a Go of Moving Abroad by

Paul Jenner and Christian Smith (ISBN: 978 0954821906) is essential reading for every potential expat. It addresses all of the typical rose-tinted dreams of wannabe migrants and dishes up a valuable dose of reality. It's not a book designed to put anybody off – more as a reality check.

Should I Stay or Should I Go? by Paul Allen (ISBN: 978 1907498008) delivers more of the same and, to be frank, I don't think that's a bad thing. In tight economic times moving abroad is a huge decision and one that may not be as easy to reverse as it was five years ago. Money spent on a reality check is money well spent.

Tales from a Travelling Mum by Alice Griffin (ISBN: 978 1905430734) isn't, strictly speaking, a moving abroad book, but I include it here as it is invaluable reading for anyone travelling or moving with young children. Alongside her engaging narrative, Alice provides many useful tips for travelling with kids in a stress-free way and the book was much appreciated by friends of ours who brought their 8-month-old son here to Portugal for his first holiday.

Speaking Portuguese

There is no end of Portuguese language-learning books, so I have concentrated here on those that have worked for us.

Teach Yourself Complete Portuguese by Manuela Cook (ISBN: 978 1444107685) was the first course we used, and having the CD in the car over a period of time was what taught us to deal competently with greetings, shops and restaurants. It's been modernised and revamped since we used it too.

Earworms Portuguese by Marlon Lodge (ISBN: 978 1905443086) is a bit different, as it uses music to drum in basic words and phrases – well worth importing to an iPod for walks and runs.

BBC Active Portuguese by Cristina Mendes-Llewellyn (ISBN: 978 0563520252) is our Portuguese tutor's book of choice and follows a good, logical way of teaching the language, similar to how you may have learned languages at school.

501 Portuguese Verbs by J. Nitti and M. Ferreira (ISBN: 978 0764129162) is essential once you get a little further down the line. It's hard work and heavy going and more of a reference book than a course, but with a language with so many irregular verbs, it is a necessary purchase.

Essential Portuguese Grammar by Alexender Da. R Prista (ISBN: 978 0486216508) is another must and probably the book we now refer to the most.

Rosetta Stone (ISBN: 978 1617166693) is the big-daddy of language courses, and those with the money to afford it could do a lot worse – it does work and some family members have used it with good results. Note, however, that it teaches you Brazilian Portuguese – which is like learning American before moving to London.

Travel and inspiration

We are residents and not tourists, but that doesn't mean we don't need guidebooks, both to learn about our own area and for when we go exploring.

AA Keyguide Portugal (ISBN: 978 0749562359) is probably my favourite of all. We constantly refer back to it, primarily because it includes some fantastic car tours and walks which are great for getting a quick sense of a new area.

DK Top 10 Algarve by Paul Bernhardt (ISBN: 978 1405360876) is another favourite, as much for the design and layout as for the information. We tend to get one of this series whenever we visit somewhere new.

DK Eyewitness Travel Guide to Portugal by Martin Symington (ISBN: 978 1405368926) is also a great choice, and was updated in June 2012 – I will be ordering the new version myself soon.

The Rough Guide to Portugal by Fisher, Hancock & Brown (ISBN: 978 1848364349) is also frequently thumbed in our house, but it seems to me to be a little overdue for an update right now.

Walking in the Algarve by Julie Statham and June Parker (ISBN: 978 1852844370) is a must for the active and was heavily used when my niece visited to train for the 3-Peaks challenge in the UK.

Living in Portugal by Anne de Stoop (ISBN: 978 2080304858) is in a category all of its own and is my one Portugal-related "coffee table book". It contains loads of history and some gorgeous photography. Before we moved here it may us feel extremely wistful!

Food and drink

I could write about foodie books all day long, so this section has been intentionally kept short to only include my favourites!

The Wine and Food Lover's Guide to Portugal by Charles Metcalfe and Kathryn McWhirter (ISBN: 978 0955706905) is a beautiful book and contains information on vineyards, restaurants and speciality dishes in each area. This book was my constant companion when the days running up to our move date seemed to drag on for ever.

Piri Piri Starfish by Tessa Kiros (ISBN: 978 1740459099) was a gift from my niece and is my favourite Portuguese cook book. As well as beautiful black and white photography it includes lots of inspiring writing about Portuguese food along with the recipes.

Lonely Planet's World Food Portugal by Lynelle Scott-Aitken and Clara de Macedo Vitorino (ISBN: 978 1864501117) is fabulous and includes historical information, a Portuguese food glossary, details on regional specialities and a scattering of recipes. As far as I can work out, the book is now out of print, so I would suggest grabbing one of the handful of second hand copies still available via Amazon.

More Portugal reading

The First Global Village by Martin Page (ISBN: 978 9724613130) is a really easy to read and engaging tome on Portuguese history – and that is coming from someone who usually sticks to the five page historical round-ups in the back of the guidebooks! Amazon has the book, but it is pricey – for those visiting Faro airport, they have it cheaper in the newsagents in departures!

Night Train to Lisbon by Pascal Mercier (ISBN: 978 1843547136) gets a mention here as it is one of few English language books set in Portugal. It is a soulful, poetic book that my wife enjoyed, as did several members of our book club – it didn't really float my boat though, to be honest.

A Small Death in Lisbon by Robert Wilson (ISBN: 978 0007322152) is a more engaging choice, in my opinion, and based on its "Gold Dagger" award for best crime novel I'm not alone. Perfect for providing a sense of atmosphere whilst on a sunlounger!

Nobody's Son by Maria Serpa (ISBN: 978 1419612824) is less well known, but comes on recommendation from my wife. We were approached to review the book and she enjoyed the romantic tale centred around a child abandoned at birth on the Portuguese island of Pico, in the Azores. The book has a somewhat quirky translation but is well worth a read, even for those not usually attracted to romantic novels.

Acknowledgements

Ben would like to say thank you to:

- Lou, for making everything possible
- His mother, for always being there and always encouraging
- Chris, for helping with the book and for making his mother so secure and happy
- Louise's family – for filling the gaps in his own and for being so welcoming
- Jard – for working really hard to keep friendship strong over such a distance
- Friends and family (especially those who have visited) for sharing an adventure and providing some of the happiest times in Portugal so far
- Anne and Nico – both for making drinks and being welcoming
- The haters and the doubters – for providing determination to make things work
- The UK ruling class and Transport for London – for making us consistently angry enough to want to escape

ACKNOWLEDGEMENTS

Louise would like to say thank you to:

- Ben, for saying "I wish we could live in Portugal" all those years ago
- Her family, for teaching her that happiness is more important than money
- Her employer, for having the foresight to see the advantages of a remote working arrangement
- Dionne, for cleaning the bathroom on the last day in England when there was so much still left to do
- The British climate for being miserable enough to inspire us to do something about it
- All the family and friends who have visited and shared our new life with us
- Portugal, for letting us live our dream

Index